A Kiss A Day

77 Days in the Love of God from The Song of Songs

by

Jamie Lash

Let Him kiss me with the kisses of His mouth: for Thy love is better than wine.

Song of Solomon 1:2

**A Kiss A Day: 77 Days in the Love of God
from The Song of Songs**

The opening quotation for each meditation is from the King James Version of the Bible. Most other quotations are from the New King James Version of the Bible © copyright 1979, 1980, 1982 by Thomas Nelson, Inc. References marked NIV are from the New International Version of the Bible, © copyright 1973, 1978, 1984 by International Bible Society, Colorado Springs, Colorado. References marked AMPLI-FIED are from the Amplified Bible, © copyright 1987 by the Zondervan Corporation and the Lockman Foundation, La Habra Foundation, California. References marked MASO-RETIC TEXT are from the Holy Scriptures According to the Masoretic Text, © copyright 1917, 1945, 1955 by The Jewish Publication Society of America. All rights reserved.

In order to capture more of the Jewish flavor, the Hebrew name for Jesus, Yeshua, has been freely substituted in most of the scriptures quoted. Similarly, the word Messiah is often substituted for Christ since both mean the "Anointed One."

Published by:

Jewish Jewels

P.O. Box 450550
Ft. Lauderdale, FL 33345-0550

ISBN 978-0-915775-07-1

First Edition: April 1996
Second Edition: September 1996
Third Edition: April 2004
Fourth Edition: September 2012

Printed in the United States of America
For Worldwide Distribution

Acknowledgments

I deeply appreciate the many people who have helped make this book possible: the faithful staff and partners of *Jewish Jewels*, our wonderful "Prayer Roses," and "bridal-souls" around the country. They have all encouraged me in my pursuit of God and my efforts to write about bridal love. My vision of the Bride of Messiah and what it means to truly love God was nurtured and expanded by the writings of Basilea Schlink and her wonderful coworkers. May the Lord richly reward each one who has helped me along the way.

Special thanks is due to Professor Timothy Rohde, Marty Koelner, Carol Washburn, Martha Barkman, Ted Dallow, Wendy Wood, and Rebecca Vitkus for their help in editing and refining the manuscript.

I am especially grateful to our gifted friend and Amish-Mennonite artist, Freiman Fisher Stoltzfus, for the cover design and artwork. Last but not least, I thank God for my husband, Neil, who loves me as Messiah loves His Bride and has consistently encouraged me to invest my talents in the Kingdom of God.

Foreword

This daily devotional is written with one goal in mind: to draw you into the love of God. We live in a day when iniquity abounds, a day spoken of in Holy Scriptures when the love of many is waxing cold: love of God, love of family, love of friends, love of country, and love of strangers, souls who may never have heard the Good News of salvation through the Messiah, Jesus.

The flame of love must be rekindled! The spark is found in our relationship with the One who loved us so much that He laid down His life for us. I call Him by His Hebrew name, *Yeshua*, the name by which He was known as a child in Nazareth and later as a teacher throughout the land of Israel. You may be accustomed to His English name, Jesus. Both names will be used throughout this devotional.

Yeshua and His relationship to the individual soul for whom He died (collectively known as the "Bride of Messiah") is the theme of a little book of only eight chapters found in the middle of the Bible. Its English name is The Song of Solomon. Its Hebrew name, and the one I prefer, is The Song of Songs.

The Song of Songs has long been a favorite book of the Jewish people. It is one of the five *megillot* or scrolls in traditional Judaism and is read on every Sabbath and at Passover in observant Jewish homes. Many Jewish people have a verse from The Song of Songs engraved on their wedding bands. Jews consider this book to be a love story about God and His people, Israel.

And so we have two love stories, two covenant peoples, one God, and one book of the Bible that has been somewhat of a mystery throughout the ages to the Church as evidenced by the scarce mention of it, despite scriptures such as 2 Timothy 3:16, which states that *all* scripture is given by

God so that the people of God might be complete. Why has this book been ignored? Because it is the most difficult book in the Old Testament to interpret, perhaps the most difficult in the entire Bible. Concerning no other book are there such differences of opinion and such a variety of interpretations.

My interpretation is very much like the earliest interpretations of The Song that prevailed throughout Jewish and Christian circles for many centuries; however, there will always be tremendous variety in the interpretation of individual verses because this book has an element of divinely-ordained subjectivity. Please use my analysis as a springboard for your own revelation from God. This is an intensely personal book—about you and *Yeshua*!

A daily journey through chapters 1 and 2 of The Song of Songs will help you move on toward spiritual maturity and a closer relationship with the Lord. You will explore the depths and heights of His love. You will experience precious union and communion with the Beloved. Your heart will be adorned with bridal love for the King of kings and the Lord of lords. Finally, you will feast on spiritual meat that will help prepare you, as part of the Bride of Messiah, to be ready and spotless when *Yeshua* comes to take you home.

Has The Song of Songs been a closed book to you? This is the time that God wants to give you the key to open it, one verse at a time, even one phrase at a time. Spiritual growth and maturity, as well as a deeper revelation of God's love for *you*, can be yours as you enter in!

The Song of Songs

Chapter One

(1) The song of songs, which is Solomon's.

(2) Let him kiss me with the kisses of his mouth: for thy love is better than wine.

(3) Because of the savour of thy good ointments thy name is as ointment poured forth, therefore do the virgins love thee.

(4) Draw me, we will run after thee: the king hath brought me into his chambers: we will be glad and rejoice in thee, we will remember thy love more than wine: the upright love thee.

(5) I am black, but comely, O ye daughters of Jerusalem, as the tents of Kedar, as the curtains of Solomon.

(6) Look not upon me, because I am black, because the sun hath looked upon me: my mother's children were angry with me; they made me the keeper of the vineyards; but mine own vineyard have I not kept.

(7) Tell me, O thou whom my soul loveth, where thou feedest, where thou makest thy flock to rest at noon: for why should I be as one that turneth aside by the flocks of thy companions?

(8) If thou know not, O thou fairest among women, go thy way forth by the footsteps of the flock, and feed thy kids beside the shepherds' tents.

(9) I have compared thee, O my love, to a company of horses in Pharaoh's chariots.

(10) Thy cheeks are comely with rows of jewels, thy neck with chains of gold.

(11) We will make thee borders of gold with studs of silver.

(12) While the king sitteth at his table, my spikenard sendeth forth the smell thereof.

(13) A bundle of myrrh is my wellbeloved unto me; he shall lie all night betwixt my breasts.

(14) My beloved is unto me as a cluster of camphire in the vineyards of Engedi.

(15) Behold, thou art fair, my love; behold, thou art fair; thou hast doves' eyes.

(16) Behold, thou art fair, my beloved, yea, pleasant: also our bed is green.

(17) The beams of our house are cedar, and our rafters of fir.

The Song of Songs
Chapter Two

(1) I am the rose of Sharon, and the lily of the valleys.

(2) As the lily among thorns, so is my love among the daughters.

(3) As the apple tree among the trees of the wood, so is my beloved among the sons. I sat down under his shadow with great delight, and his fruit was sweet to my taste.

(4) He brought me to the banqueting house, and his banner over me was love.

(5) Stay me with flagons, comfort me with apples: for I am sick of love.

(6) His left hand is under my head, and his right hand doth embrace me.

(7) I charge you, O ye daughters of Jerusalem, by the roes, and by the hinds of the field, that ye stir not up, nor awake my love, till he please.

(8) The voice of my beloved! behold, he cometh leaping upon the mountains, skipping upon the hills.

(9) My beloved is like a roe or a young hart: behold, he standeth behind our wall, he looketh forth at the windows, shewing himself through the lattice.

(10) My beloved spake, and said unto me, Rise up, my love, my fair one, and come away.

(11) For, lo, the winter is past, the rain is over and gone;

(12) The flowers appear on the earth; the time of the singing of birds is come, and the voice of the turtle[dove] is heard in our land;

(13) The fig tree putteth forth her green figs, and the vines with the tender grape give a good smell. Arise, my love, my fair one, and come away.

(14) O my dove, that art in the clefts of the rock, in the secret places of the stairs, let me see thy countenance, let me hear thy voice; for sweet is thy voice, and thy countenance is comely.

(15) Take us the foxes, the little foxes, that spoil the vines: for our vines have tender grapes.

(16) My beloved is mine, and I am his: he feedeth among the lilies.

(17) Until the day break, and the shadows flee away, turn, my beloved, and be thou like a roe or a young hart upon the mountains of Bether.

A Word About Textual Divisions

All together there are eight chapters in The Song of Songs. Bible scholars throughout the ages have proposed various divisions or stages in the text. *The New Scofield Reference Bible* divides The Song into thirteen canticles or songs. Irving L. Jensen uses three main divisions: courtship days, wedding, and married life. Watchman Nee divides The Song into five parts: initial love, faltering love, growing love, transforming love and mature love. Hudson Taylor proposes six sections. Coral Harris Mac Ilravy writes about five canticles or songs within The Song: 1:1-2:7, 2:8-3:5, 3:6-5:1, 5:2-8:5, and 8:5-14. Many other divisions have been postulated.

The vast majority of Bible scholars agree on one thing: There is a definite *progression* in The Song of Songs, from love's first stirring to mature, bridal love. There is a process involved that includes times of togetherness and times of separation. There are times when the Bridegroom is present (represented by *day*) and times when He is absent (represented by *night*).

I tend to think of The Song in terms of the three confessions of the Bride that represent three levels of maturity: *"My beloved is mine and I am his"* (2:16), *"I am my beloved's and my beloved is mine"* (6:3), and *"I am my beloved's and his desire is toward me"* (7:10). Three divisions can also be found if the eight chapters are grouped together as follows: chapters 1 and 2, "First Love"; 3 through 5, "Wilderness Love"; and 6 through 8, "Invincible Love."

You may discover yet another pattern in The Song of Songs, for it is a many-faceted jewel. **Enjoy your adventure!**

Day 1

The song of songs...   Song of Songs 1:1

The Holy Scriptures are filled with songs: the song of
Moses (Deuteronomy 32:1-43), Hannah's song (1 Samuel
2:1-10), the entire book of Psalms, and Mary's song (Luke
1:46-55), just to name a few. Some musicologists have even
speculated that the entire Bible was originally set to music.
If this were indeed true, it would accentuate the already
great significance of the use of the Hebrew superlative in
the title of the tiny but precious biblical jewel that God
wants to place in our hands this year, The Song of Songs.

Shir HaShirim is the Hebrew for Song of Songs. Just as
Lord of lords means *the Supreme Lord,* and *King of kings, the
Supreme King, The Song of Songs* means *the supreme song* or
the most excellent of all songs. Whose opinion is this? God's!
It is not only His opinion, but His musical taste, and a
reflection of who He is.

What makes this song the best one of all? Its theme:
LOVE. There's nothing greater than love. It is the only
thing, according to the New Covenant equivalent to The
Song of Songs—1 Corinthians 13—that never fails. God *is*
Love, a love that puts music in the heart. His favorite song
could be none other than a song of love.

And yet, there was much controversy about The Song of
Songs when the biblical canon was decided upon. Many
were of the opinion that The Song of Songs should not be
included in the Holy Scriptures. When read on a purely
literal level, the love song is often graphically sensual and
mundane. In the Jewish tradition, it was forbidden to read
The Song of Songs until the age of thirty.

Rabbi Akiva, a highly renowned Jewish sage, defended
the book and was instrumental in its inclusion in the Holy

Scriptures. He is said to have made the following statement: "...for the whole world existed, so to speak, for the day on which The Song of Songs was given to it. Why so? Because all the writings are holy, and this is holy of holies."

This has been my personal experience. The Song of Songs has ushered me, time and time again, into the very presence of God. From 1980 through 1985, I spent a minimum of two hours each day studying and meditating on The Song. In 1982, the revelation of the relationship that God was bringing me into moved from my spirit to my understanding (from my heart to my head), and I was able to begin sharing with others the treasures I had found. The greatest revelation God gave me during that time is that *I am in The Song of Songs! I* am the object of the greatest love in the universe.

This is the revelation that God wants to impart to *your* spirit. It will revolutionize your life and will enable you to enter into the mutual love, two-way communication, dual-holiness, and reciprocal praises that are all a part of The Song of Songs.

Are you ready for a great adventure in God?

Ask Him to bring you into His holy of holies.

You have a place in The Song of Songs!

Day 2

Solomon, *Shlomo* in Hebrew, is generally considered to be the author of The Song of Songs. The Bible tells us in 1 Kings 4:32 that Solomon wrote 1,005 songs altogether, this one being his most excellent. *Shlomo* literally means *Peace is his.* The Lord had told Solomon's father, David, that his son's reign would be one of peace, *shalom* (1 Chronicles 22:9).

In traditional Jewish thought, *Shlomo* represents the God of Abraham, Isaac, and Jacob, the Lover of Israel. According to the allegorical Christian interpretation of The Song (to which I ascribe), Solomon represents our Messiah/ King, our Heavenly Bridegroom or Prince of Peace, *Yeshua HaMashiach*, Jesus the Messiah.

Although he was a great and wise king, Solomon set his affection upon a simple country girl. She was *the Shulamite,* which literally means *Peace is hers.* Their relationship parallels that of a believer and the Lord *Yeshua,* as well as God's relationship to Israel. Who is little Israel that the Master of the whole universe should set His love upon her? And who are *we* that *Yeshua,* the King of Glory, should choose us as His beloved Bride? The answer to these questions is not found in us, but rather in *Him.*

When I first began studying The Song of Songs in 1980, there was another question that disturbed me greatly. How could God allow Solomon to represent the Lord of Heaven when the Bible makes it clear that Solomon had hundreds of wives and concubines who turned his heart away from the Lord at the end of his life (1 Kings 11:3-4)?

While praying about this, I began to think about myself and the millions of others like me who are ambassadors of

Messiah, bearing the name of the Kings of kings and Lord of lords. Certainly, we are not worthy of the treasure that has been entrusted to us! After a time of silence, I sensed the Holy Spirit speak a direct word to my spirit:

"Solomon was called to be a lover of God in the Spirit. At the end of his life, his calling was corrupted, and he went from the Spirit to the flesh. Find a prostitute, a homosexual, someone who is very much given over to sexual promiscuity, and you'll find someone whose true calling is to be *a lover of God*. Redirect them!"

Perhaps this insight will enable you to speak life to someone near you. Perhaps you were involved in promiscuous behavior before coming to the Lord and never understood the devil's tactics to derail you from your true calling as a lover of God. Get on track. The best is yet to come!

God wants to fill you with a song this year. The song is Solomon's (God's). It begins with Him. He initiates every action. He is always the One who chooses first, whether it be Israel or His Bride. Messiah said, in John 15:16, *"You did not choose Me, but I chose you."* We love God *because He first loved us* (1 John 4:19).

Shlomo HaMelech, Solomon the King, was given riches, power, wisdom, a reign of peace, and royal majesty unlike any other king of Israel (1 Chronicles 29:25). But there is a King who surpasses Solomon in every way. *Yeshua* Himself proclaimed, *"…a greater than Solomon is here"* (Luke 11:31).

Yeshua is our *Shlomo*. He is a mighty King, and He is in love with you.

His wisdom is yours.

His riches are yours.

His authority is yours.

His heart is yours.

And He has called *you* to be a lover of God!

Day 3

He will joy [rejoice] over thee with singing.
Zephaniah 3:17

Does God sing? How well do we really know Him? Do we merely know His acts, or do we know His ways, as Moses did (Psalm 103:7)? If love gives birth to song and God is love, then surely He must sing!

From time to time, in *A Kiss A Day*, I will be using related verses from the Old and New Covenant Scriptures that amplify or help to clarify The Song. Such is the case with our verse for today.

This verse from the prophet Zephaniah helps to clarify Song of Songs 1:1. God rejoices over us with singing. Have you ever been soothed by a song? This will be your experience as the Lord sings His favorite song over you. You have brought joy to the Father's heart by just being YOU.

Earthly parents sing over their little ones while rocking them to sleep or while putting them to bed. How much more must God, our Heavenly Father, sing over us! When my oldest son Jonathan was making his own music inside of me (mainly at night with lots of percussion-like moves), I was overwhelmed with love for this little person whom I'd never seen. That love gave birth to a song. The tune was simple, and a portion of the lyrics are as follows:

> *Can you love anyone you've never seen?*
> *Yes, you can!*
> *Can they really be real, listen and feel?*
> *Yes, they can!*
> *For a baby's a person, even in his mother.*
> *And God is a person too, just like no other.*
> *He knew each of us before we were born,*
> *and He fashioned us in love...*

5

After having the wonderful experience of pregnancy and bringing forth life, I can imagine God singing over each new spiritual baby born into the Kingdom of God. If the angels rejoice (Luke 15:10), think how much more the Father rejoices! I believe that God also sings over each physical baby that is born, a new, little soul made in His image with the capacity to love and be loved. This is precious to the heart of God.

After two years of rejoicing with singing over my firstborn, I was astonished and delighted to find him rejoicing over *me* in our living room one afternoon. It was close to *Hanukkah* 1987, and Jonathan, filled with the holiday spirit, was singing and dancing to holiday music. All of a sudden, with great joy and exuberance, he began exclaiming, "Glory to Mama in the highest!" At that moment I caught a glimpse of how our Heavenly Father feels when we rejoice in Him.

This kind of spontaneous, joyous, wonderful love flows from the heart of God to each of His children at all times and in all seasons. He is singing over us today. We must fine tune our ears to hear Him! The truth is, God deeply cares about each of His children! *Yeshua* is madly in love with His Bride!

The prophet Isaiah expressed it this way: *"As a bridegroom rejoices over his bride, so will your God rejoice over you"* (Isaiah 62:5 NIV).

It's true. He loves you.

Day 4

I am thy shield, and thy exceeding great reward.
Genesis 15:1

It was February 14, and the word *love* was passing through checkout counters at an amazing rate of speed. "Love," usually mistaken for lust in America today, is the central theme of Valentine's Day in our country. I went home to my piano that day, sat down, and began talking to the Lord. I expressed to Him that I was so grateful to have found real love, *His* kind of love, unconditional, eternal, sacrificial love. My heart was bursting with the revelation of the greatness of the love of God, and I desired to express my love to Him.

Genesis 15:1 came to mind with the wonderful promise that God gave to Abram, assuring him of not only protection but also great blessing. God promised to be Abram's reward. What reward would be meaningful to you today? A raise? A promotion? A scholarship? A word of praise, encouragement, or thanks? A new home? A car? A job? We generally don't think of *God* Himself as being a reward. But more of Him and His presence in our lives is the very best reward there is!

A simple melody came to mind to which I put words in a matter of seconds:

I love you.
I love you.
I love you, Lord.
I love you.
I love you.
YOU are my reward.

I continued to play this little love song to the Lord over

and over, as tears were streaming down my face. Then I heard a voice gently singing back to me, in a kind of counterpoint. I stopped abruptly and said out loud, "Does God sing?"

No sooner had I formed the question on my lips than the answer came in the form of a Scripture verse: Zephaniah 3:17 (see yesterday's devotion). I shouted out, "Yes, You do sing, Lord!"

He continued with His part of the song:

> *Stay! Stay! I love you this way,*
> *Resting in My love, and hearing from above.*
> *Stay! Stay! I love you this way.*
> *There's more that I have yet to say...*

I tarried in His presence for quite a while. When my husband Neil came home from work that day, I called him to the piano and excitedly told him that God had given me a little "Valentine" song, and Neil had to sing God's part! (Neil says that this was one of the most awesome challenges I have ever presented him with.)

God bids us to "stay" a while longer with Him, to sit at His feet, to listen to His voice. As we *rest in His love*, we will *hear from above*. Perhaps you can stay a little longer with the Lord today. Nothing pleases His heart more. *Yeshua*'s words in the garden, *"Could you not watch with Me one hour?"*, prick my spirit today. He is the *rewarder of those who diligently seek Him. There's more that He has yet to say.*

Day 5

Let him kiss me with the kisses of his mouth.
Song of Songs 1:2

This is the cry of the "bride spirit" — a desire for more of the Beloved, a desire for intimacy. The Shulamite maiden (Israel, the Bride of Messiah, the individual soul for whom Messiah died) is speaking here. She is not satisfied with relationship at a distance. She desires close contact. Kissing only occurs in close, face-to-face relationships.

The Holy Scriptures tell us that God spoke to Moses *p'anim el p'anim,* face to face. He spoke to the people of Israel at various times and in different ways throughout the prophets. But in these last days, He has spoken to us *by His Son, Yeshua* (Hebrews 1:1-2).

What exactly is a kiss from God? According to rabbinic tradition, it is a living word of prophecy. The Christian equivalent would be a *rhema* word. Have you ever had the experience of reading or hearing something from the Bible that suddenly came alive to you, literally jumping off the page, and you knew that God was speaking to *you*? If you have, you've been kissed by God! There's nothing quite like having direct contact with the Creator. This is the epitome of all communication. It is what we were created for.

We must yearn for this direct communion with God, in the same way that pious Jews throughout the centuries have yearned for the coming of the Messiah. They await His coming — and His kiss. We must tell God's people, Israel, that He has already come, and will kiss them as they receive Him by faith. *Yeshua* Himself *is* a kiss from God to Israel and the nations.

Jewish sources often quote Deuteronomy 18:18 when commenting on the kisses of God: *"I will raise up for them a Prophet like you from among their brethren, and will put My words in His mouth, and He shall speak to them all that I command Him."* They conclude that the phrase *kisses of his mouth (Song of Songs 1:2)* refers to prophecy. This is true in part. The rest of the truth is that the Prophet like Moses whom God raised up is *Yeshua*, Jesus of Nazareth, the One who came to do the will of the Father and only did (or spoke) those things that He saw His Father doing (John 5:19).

Do you long to hear from God, to be kissed by Him? It is His desire to give you a kiss a day, or as many kisses as you will receive. *Yeshua's* kisses are life-giving. The Bible tell us, in Deuteronomy 8:3, that *"Man shall not live by bread alone; but man lives by every word that proceeds from the mouth of the Lord."* In other words, we live by kisses from God.

Receive a kiss by going to your Bible today. If you haven't already begun a regular pattern of Bible reading, now is the time to begin. Start with a chapter a day. Be faithful. Be consistent. Read God's Word with a sense of expectancy, a desire to be kissed, and confidence in the promise from John 10:27, *"My sheep hear My voice, and I know them, and they follow Me."*

Brothers in the Lord, this includes you, too. You are part of the mystical "Bride of Messiah." Let each of us go to our prayer closet today with Bible in hand. Let us look up into the face of *Yeshua*, our Heavenly Bridegroom, and say, "You may kiss the Bride!"

𝒟ay 6

Righteousness and peace kiss each other.
Psalm 85:10 (NIV)

When do righteousness and peace kiss? When an individual believer has intimate communion with the Prince of Peace (Isaiah 9:6). Consider the following two scriptures as a backdrop to this conclusion:

2 Corinthians 5:21: *"For He [God] made Him [Yeshua] who knew no sin to be sin for us, that WE might become the RIGHTEOUSNESS of God in Him."*

Ephesians 2:14: *"For HE Himself is OUR PEACE, who has made both one, and has broken down the middle wall of separation..."*

We need to see ourselves as God sees us — as the righteousness of God *in Messiah*. Our opinion of ourselves should agree with God's opinion, not with the devil's (he is quick to enumerate all our faults and weaknesses). While it is true that all *our* righteousness is as filthy rags (Isaiah 64:6), we no longer stand in our own goodness. We have been imparted righteousness, which is right standing with God, because of who *Yeshua* is and what He did for us. What a gift! How thankful we should be.

We are righteous by faith in the Son of God. Righteousness by faith goes all the way back to Abraham who *believed* in the Lord, and God accounted it to him for righteousness (Genesis 15:6). God wants us to know who we are *in Him* and to teach this truth to our children. When we are right with God, we have been fulfilled, whether Jew or non-Jew. Ours is a position of contentment! With God as our Father and *Yeshua* as our Savior, we have all we need. *"Better is a little with righteousness, than vast revenues without justice"* (Proverbs 16:8). Righteousness, not possessions, power, or position, is the real treasure.

A few months *before* accepting *Yeshua* as my Savior, the Lord gave me *a kiss* from Isaiah 42:6. (Don't assume that God can only kiss believers!) I knew it was the God of Abraham, Isaac, and Jacob speaking to me about Neil and myself and our future in Him: *"I, the LORD, have called You in righteousness, and will hold Your hand. I will keep You and give you as a covenant to the people, as a light to the Gentiles."*

We were once unrighteous. Now we have been called in righteousness by One who holds our hand! He is so wonderful. He is our PEACE. In our particular family, we live in the reality of Ephesians 2:14. I was not born into a Jewish family. My husband, Neil, was. In the Messiah, we are beautifully one, Jew and non-Jew, male and female. In our ministry there is no division between the *Tanach* (Old Covenant) and the *Brit HaDasha* (New Covenant). It is all one Bible. The middle wall of partition has been broken down. Where there was division, there is now unity. Where there was conflict, there is now *shalom shalom*, perfect peace. *Yeshua* is the answer to the Jew/non-Jew struggles that permeate so many families today. He brings peace because He *is* peace.

When we're rightly related to the *Sar Shalom, the Prince of Peace,* we can experience a peace that passes understanding. Whatever your life circumstances may be, remember you are the *Shulamite* and your name means *Peace is hers.* Is peace a quality that is obvious in your life? Let *Yeshua* minister His perfect peace — *Shalom Shalom* — to your heart today. God is in control.

$\mathcal{D}ay$ 7

Kiss the Son... Blessed are all they that put their trust in Him. Psalm 2:12

This is another good example of "kissing" from the *Tanach* (Old Covenant Scriptures). Most Jewish people today have never read Psalm 2:12, don't know that it is a "Messianic Psalm," and aren't even aware that the Bible says that God has a son in verses such as Psalm 2:12 and Proverbs 30:4. They are familiar, however, with various religious practices that involve kissing because, in traditional Judaism, kissing is an act of religious devotion.

The Torah (first five books of the Law) is kissed by worshippers (actually, one touches the Torah mantle and then kisses one's fingers) when it is carried in a synagogue procession as an act of worship, and in reverence for the Word of God.

Many Jews follow the custom of touching the *mezuzah* (a small box on the doorpost of Jewish homes which contains Scripture verses) with the fingertips, kissing them, and reciting, "May God protect my going out and coming in, now and forever." The fringes of the *talit*, or prayer shawl, are kissed when it is put on. When a holy book (prayer book or Bible) is dropped, it is kissed after it has been picked up from the ground.

But the real kiss that the God of Abraham, Isaac, and Jacob longs for from His Jewish people is the one spoken of in Psalm 2:12. *Kiss the Son!*

Ely and Joan, both raised in Conservative Jewish homes, kissed the Son on November 6, 1995, as they prayed together to receive *Yeshua* as their Messiah and Lord. Jewish people all over the world are beginning to kiss the Son. Each has a testimony of God's special way of drawing them unto Himself.

Ely and Joan are no exception. Their story is a very beautiful one. I'd like to share a portion of it in their own words. Following are excerpts from the seventeen-page letter they sent to Joan's Jewish mother and brother on November 20, 1995, informing them of their acceptance of *Yeshua* as their Messiah. The letter included the history of their search for God, their decision for *Yeshua*, and a six-page bibliography with suggestions, resources, and references.

We have recently made the most important decision based upon months of study and research and deep soul searching. It was not a decision we made easily or without great thought or emotional turmoil... We have had outstanding Jewish upbringings. Since we married, we have continued to keep Kosher and to celebrate the Jewish holidays. Even though we have belonged to Conservative synagogues, we began to feel that something was "missing" from our spiritual lives.

Joan happened to spot a TV program on Saturdays called "Jewish Jewels." When she started to watch the show, Neil and Jamie, the hosts, talked about Yeshua being the Jewish Messiah. Joan immediately would flip to another channel. During one of the Friday night services at the Reform synagogue, when the Rabbi was out of town, a guest speaker, an "anti-missionary," spoke. He spoke about "Jewish Jewels" and cautioned people NOT to become involved with such a group.

Now, when someone tells you NOT to do something, it can help to peak your curiosity even more! The next day, we tuned into" Jewish Jewels" and watched the show from start to finish. With an OPEN mind, we listened to the hosts. With an OPEN mind, we started to watch the program religiously from that day forward. In addition to the weekly programs we watch on TV, we have read many books and articles and viewed videotapes on various subjects.

The real importance of our decision to accept Yeshua as the Jewish Messiah lies in our relationship with God. We feel that we now have a very real, very personal relationship with God.

14

Hallelujah! Relationship, not religion, is God's will for all. Ely and Joan are now Messianic Jews. They have put their trust in *Yeshua,* and they are blessed. Ely told us the other day that God gave him his first kiss. This verse from the Holy Scriptures has become the bedrock of his relationship with God: *"Come now, and let us reason together, says the Lord..."* (Isaiah 1:18). As a scientist, Ely was deeply touched by the willingness of the Creator of the Universe to dialogue with man. As a Jew, he felt as if he had come home.

Pray for your Jewish friends and neighbors, and share God's Word with them. He is removing the veil from their hearts and the scales from their eyes and revealing their Messiah to them.

Day 8

For thy love is better than wine.
Song of Songs 1:2

Wine, *yayin* in Hebrew, was very much a part of daily life for the people of Spain among whom I lived for two years while studying to be a Spanish teacher. When someone spilled wine at the table they always said, *"Alegria,"* which means *pleasure* or *rejoicing.* The kind of joy that comes from wine is profane, worldly joy. It is temporary, superficial, and proceeds from the flesh. Wine is used in The Song of Songs to represent this physical gratification. It symbolizes the pleasures of the world and their intoxicating effect on those who pursue them.

The world indeed does offer pleasure, and sin is pleasant for a season, but there is definitely a higher and a better way to live. Many of us who have come to the Messiah as adults have, unfortunately, tasted the "wine" and can say from experience: God's love is better than wine! His love is greater than *anything* the world has to offer.

God's divine love, *ahavah* in Hebrew, ministers to the spirit. It is a self-sacrificing, eternally-giving, unconditional love, unlike man's kind of love. Our love fails, but God's does not. My life scripture verse is 1 Corinthians 13:8: *"Love never fails."* I had the great fortune of growing up in a family with a loving, affirming mother and a father who adored me and called me his "princess."

At the age of 26 I received *Yeshua* (Jesus, to me then) as my Savior after about a year of being wooed by the Spirit of God. Wooed? Yes, I literally sensed a powerful *love* drawing me to a new life, a life in God. I would listen for hours to a Christian record album by a group called Love

16

Song and weep with joy at the love I felt reaching out to me. I experienced the same thing when I picked up a Bible, especially when reading the book of John.

Over a period of about a year, I began to fall in love with the person of *Yeshua*, the Messiah. I had known a lot of love in my life. I came from a loving family, and was married to a very loving man, but I had *never* experienced a love like this. This love was worth giving up everything for. It was the *pearl of great price* to me.

From the day of my new birth until now, I have never seen God as anything but Love, nor have I ever desired to go back to the world. The love of God is amazing, awesome, irresistible, dependable, passionate, and persistent. It is always there for us, even in the most tragic circumstances — death, divorce, terminal illness, accidents, betrayals, abuse. None of these change the fact that God is love and that His love is the greatest power in Heaven and earth.

Are you having a hard time receiving the love of God? Talk to Him about it. Ask God to reveal His love and His Father's heart to you. God is no respecter of persons. He desires with all His heart for you to experience the holy joy (far greater than *alegria*; I would call it *gozo profundo*, a deep joy) that comes from receiving the love that's *better than wine*.

$\mathcal{D}ay$ 9

...because of the savor of thy good ointments...
Song of Songs 1:3

All the senses become involved in love — hearing the love song, tasting and touching in a kiss, and savoring the fragrance of the clothing of one's beloved. I love the smell of my husband's shirts. I also love the smell of my own blouses, scented with my favorite perfume.

During my first year at Ohio Wesleyan University, I remember wearing one of my favorite sweatshirts to bed, spraying it with my perfume the following morning, wrapping it quickly in a box, and sending it to my father in New York as a gift. I knew that when he opened the box, he would smell ME, and it would bring him great joy. It did!

Another savor that is *good* beyond description is the fragrance of a baby fresh from the bath, swaddled and new. On January 10, 1989, such a bundle was presented to me as I lay waiting in a hospital bed. Jesse Allan Lash, our second son, had come into the world smelling of life, love, and hope for the future. God sent him on the anniversary of my mother's death, and now, on every January 10th, there is the fragrance of candles in our home: a *Yahrzeit* (memorial) candle for Mother and birthday candles for Jesse.

What about the fragrance of Messiah? The Bible describes His fragrance in Psalm 45. This psalm, which is sometimes titled a "Song of Love" or a "Messianic Wedding Song," speaks of Messiah and His Bride. Both the divine character and fragrance of Messiah are referred to in verses 6-8: *"Your throne, O God, is forever and ever... therefore God, Your God, has anointed You with the oil of gladness more than Your companions. All Your garments are scented with myrrh and aloes and cassia..."*

18

According to Jewish tradition, fragrance is related to character. Myrrh speaks of *Yeshua*'s suffering and sacrificial love, aloes and cassia of the healing in His wings. All three of these spices were also found in the holy oil used to anoint the High Priest in Temple times.

Yeshua, Jesus, is our High Priest. He is the *Mashiach*, the Messiah, literally *The Anointed One*. Whereas the High Priests before Him offered up sacrifices and burned incense perpetually before the Lord on the altar of incense, *Yeshua* offered up the sacrifice of Himself as *a sweet-smelling savour to God*.

As followers of The Anointed One, we can walk in His anointing, having the oil of joy instead of mourning, and the sweetness of salvation instead of the stench of sin. We are told, in 2 Corinthians 2:15-16, that God diffuses the fragrance of the knowledge of Messiah in every place through us: *"For we are to God the fragrance of Messiah among those who are being saved and among those who are perishing. To the one we are the aroma of death [leading] to death, and to the other the aroma of life [leading] to life..."*

Be who you are. Rest in the knowledge that your fragrance delights the Father's heart. In you He detects the aroma of Bethlehem's Babe, Jerusalem's King, His precious Son.

Day 10

Thy name is as ointment poured forth.
Song of Songs 1:3

HaShem means *the Name* in Hebrew. That is how God is referred to by most Orthodox Jews today, since the Lord's name as given in the tetragrammaton, *YHWH,* is considered too holy to pronounce. There certainly is something very special, holy, praiseworthy, and to be revered about the name of God. But in His great love, the God of Abraham, Isaac, and Jacob allowed the holy to meet the profane, Heaven to touch earth, and a name to be *given* to men when He sent His only Son into the world to bring us salvation.

This name, *Yeshua* (Jesus, when translated into English), was first spoken by an angel. The name itself explained what this child would become, for *Yeshua* literally means *salvation. "And you shall call His name [Yeshua], for He will save His people from their sins"* (Matthew 1:21).

We've already seen in verse three that *Yeshua's* ointments are *good.* Likewise, His name is a *good name.* Names were very important in the Middle East during Bible times. *Your name* was a Semitic idiom for *your very self.* Everything that *Yeshua* was and is can be found in His name. There's no other name in Heaven or on earth that can compare with the name *Yeshua.* For this reason, the Bible calls it the *"name above every name"* (Philippians 2:9).

How is this wonderful name like ointment poured forth? First of all, Eastern peoples, at the time of *Yeshua,* made frequent use of fragrant ointments. These ointments were used for hospitality and for medicinal and personal purposes. Some of them were very costly. Balsam, for example, was worth double its weight in silver. Spikenard was less costly but was also considered "precious."

Oil of roses was one of the most popular and least costly of the ointments. The expression *precious* or *very precious* as applied to ointments in 2 Kings 20:13, Psalm 133:2, Ecclesiastes 7:1, Matthew 26:7, and John 12:3 shows us the high esteem given to ointments by the early Hebrews.

The name *Yeshua* is also *precious* and to be highly esteemed! Like expensive ointment, it has special virtues. As ointment was used to welcome guests, the name *Yeshua* is God's welcome to us. Without it, we are strangers. In *Yeshua*, we have found a home.

As ointment was used to anoint the sick, because of its softening, soothing properties and natural healing power, the name of *Yeshua* is a source of healing to His Bride. In His name there is power over both physical and emotional afflictions. How often we have anointed ourselves and others with oil in the name of *Yeshua* and seen the Lord heal the sick! We stand on the Word of the Lord found in James 5:14-15: *"Is anyone among you sick? Let him call for the elders of the church [congregation], and let them pray over him, anointing him with oil in the name of the Lord. And the prayer of faith will save the sick, and the Lord will raise him up."*

There would be no welcome nor healing in the name of *Yeshua* today if the ointment had not been *poured forth* nearly 2,000 years ago. On the tree of sacrifice, nails pierced the vessel that held the precious ointment. As *Yeshua* poured out His soul unto death, His name — *Salvation* — was poured forth, and the fragrance of sacrificial love spread from Jerusalem to *the uttermost parts of the earth.*

Are you hurting today?

There is welcome and healing in the name of *Yeshua*. Call upon His name. *Yeshua* is God's *yes* to you!

Day 11

Why do we love God?

In the early stages of our walk with God, we usually love Him because of what He has done for us, what He has given us. The name of *Yeshua* stands for everything that we have been given: eternal life, a new life here on earth, a relationship with God as our Father, peace that passes understanding, unconditional love, the presence of God in our lives, a Bible full of promises to claim as our very own, wisdom from above, guidance for our daily lives, healing for our bodies, and more!

All of these are manifestations of the love of God. They are *dodim*, in Hebrew, literally *caresses*. *Dodim* is the word for love that is used in verse two (*better than wine*) of The Song. Our first love experience with the Lord is based more on what He has given than on who He is. New believers are more sense-oriented and concrete than mature believers. God expects this, and I believe He delights in it.

God, after all, is both a Father and a Giver. As a Father, He derives joy from seeing His children happy. As a giver, He is fulfilled when He gives. I've always sensed that the Lord is looking for receivers — those who will please the heart of God by receiving all the gifts He has to give and then acting as a channel of blessing to others, letting the gifts flow through them and out to a needy world.

Perhaps you missed this stage. If so, go back! God wants to show you His giving heart. He wants you to learn to receive from Him — because you are His child. He loves you, and it is His good pleasure to give you the kingdom!

I'll never forget the day, as a young believer in the

Lord, that I decided to claim a promise from God's Word. I remember how excited I was to find that we could speak to mountains and they would be cast into the sea! It was right before the Passover, and I was intent on cleansing my closets, home, heart, body, my whole life from *leaven*.

I had a black mole on my face under my left eye. I decided that it was *leaven* and that it had to leave my body before Passover. Every day for a couple of weeks I would look into the mirror, curse the "face leaven," as I called it, in the name of *Yeshua*, and command the mountain to be removed. The night before Passover, the mole fell off my face into the sink right before my eyes, leaving no mark whatsoever on my face. I was ecstatic and exuberantly expressed my love to God for doing such a great work. Somehow I seemed to sense that God was laughing and getting a kick out of my childlike ways.

Who are the "virgins" of verse 3? You and I. Spiritually, we become "virgins" through *Yeshua* — pure in heart, like children, innocent, unmarred, set apart unto Him. Though our sins were *as scarlet*, He makes us *as white as snow* (another kiss from Isaiah 1:18). *Yeshua* makes us whole. How can we not love Him for forgiving us and giving us a new start?

That's the miracle of salvation. We exchange our filthy, smelly rags for His pure, fragrant righteousness! When *Yeshua* cleanses us in His blood, it is as if we had never sinned. We are unleavened. We have become, in the words of Rabbi Saul of Tarsus, a *"chaste virgin to [Messiah]"* (2 Corinthians 11:2).

Know who you are in Him! You have been washed, sanctified, and justified in the name of the Lord *Yeshua* and by the Spirit of our God (1 Corinthians 6:11). Expect great things from the Lord!

$\mathcal{D}ay$ 12

Draw me.   Song of Songs 1:4

The first two words of verse four are the cry of one who has known the love of her bridegroom, His fragrance, His name, His sacrifice on her behalf, and the vast provision included in that sacrifice. And yet, she still finds it necessary to pray *"Draw me."* And so do we!

How easy it is to become spiritually distracted, lazy, complacent, even cold in our day and age. There are so many pressures on us and even on our children, pressures that our parents and grandparents didn't have to deal with. These pressures sometimes result in neglect of our relationship with the Beloved.

Do you feel indifferent today with no desire to be drawn? Perhaps you feel spiritually dead inside. That doesn't mean that you aren't part of Messiah's Bride. I'll never forget a dream I had many years ago. I was in a room all alone. A casket was in front of me. As I approached the casket, I saw a dead bride lying in it. A voice spoke to me and said, "Lay your hands upon the bride."

I immediately said, "No!"

The voice spoke again, with great authority.

I replied, "No, I don't want to touch a dead body."

I knew at that point that God was speaking to me firmly. "I told you to lay hands on the bride," He repeated.

I answered, "What will You do if I do it?"

The Lord replied, "I am going to resurrect her!"

Are you a part of the sleeping (dead) bride? Please allow me to lay my hands on you through *A Kiss A Day*. God wants to impart divine life to you. He plans to raise you from the dead! Cry out to God, *"Draw me,"* and His Spirit will begin to move in your heart and life.

Draw me is a cry for help and it relates to spiritual hunger—the basis for growth in God. When I pray this simple, two-word prayer to the Lord, I mean, "Woo me, Lord. Heighten my desire for You. Make our relationship (the Bible, my prayer life) exciting again. Do a work in my heart. I need more of You in my life. I want to *know* Your will and *do* Your will. I want to experience Your love in its fullness."

How does God draw us to Himself? By the *Ruach HaKodesh*, His Holy Spirit. God says the following to His people, in Jeremiah 31:3: "*Yes, I have loved you with an everlasting love; therefore, with lovingkindness I have drawn you.*" The Talmud (Kiddushin 22) states that *"drawing"* is a form of establishing ownership. As the God of Abraham, Isaac, and Jacob draws us unto Himself, He is indeed saying, "She/he is mine. They belong to me."

We need to welcome the presence of the *Ruach HaKodesh* in our lives. He will draw us to our Heavenly Bridegroom with gentle cords of love (Hosea 11:4). Do not grieve the Spirit of God by what you say, what you watch on television, or who you choose as friends, but allow God's Spirit to draw you in paths of holiness instead. He will point the way to *Yeshua* and show you new truths about Him. The Holy Spirit lifts up *Yeshua*. Then *He* draws all men unto Himself (John 12:32).

Consider beginning each new day by praying "Draw me." These two little words could change your entire life.

$\mathscr{D}ay$ 13

We will run after thee.   Song of Songs 1:4

You may not be into tennis or aerobics, weight lifting or racquetball, but you are called to be a jogger — in the Spirit of God! While physical exercise does profit a little (and I really need more of it myself), the Holy Scriptures tell us that spiritual exercise brings great gain (reward).

Joggers must be disciplined. So must disciples of *Yeshua*. Oh, how hard it is to discipline the flesh! We get tired, lazy, don't feel like it, have so many other things to do, so many "excuses." And yet, there is a "best choice" — the one that Mary made as recorded in Luke 10:42. Mary chose to run after *Yeshua* — not physically, but with her heart. It's always a choice, an act of the will. There's a decision to be made and a commitment to keep, "I WILL *run after* You, Lord."

You don't need strong legs, good lungs, or a lean and healthy body to run after the Lord. In fact, some of the best spiritual joggers I know have serious illnesses and are home-bound or in wheelchairs. They have what it takes: love in their hearts for *Yeshua*, a desire to follow Him, to live for Him, and to do His will. And they make themselves available to the Lord. This is most precious. *Yeshua* wants *us*, not what we can do for Him.

This is a battle I face constantly because I am a worker, an achiever. I love to produce, to create. It is hard for me to just sit and visit. And yet, paradoxically, "running after *Yeshua*" doesn't mean so much working diligently in His service and being active in the affairs of the Kingdom as it means sitting still and letting your heart pursue Him with all that is within you.

This is what revival is really all about — a renewal of that desire to run after *Yeshua* and not to stop until you have reached the goal of His tender embrace, His life-giving kisses, intimate fellowship with Him.

Have you noticed that the bride cried, *"Draw ME, and WE will run after thee"?* Who is the *we*? *We* is the result of a ripple effect. When one member of a family, congregation, or fellowship is drawn, others will follow.

I have had the delightful experience many times over the years of being what I call "surprised by the joy of the Lord." Usually when I have least expected it (for example, four days before giving birth to Jesse), God's Spirit has been sovereignly poured out upon me from above, and I have been flooded with a supernatural joy that bursts forth from my innermost being in the form of a glorious kind of laughter. On one of these occasions, in August of 1975, I laughed in the Spirit for over an hour. Our pastor asked me to pray for the people in our congregation that they might receive the joy of the Lord also. Almost everyone I touched experienced this same special anointing. I was drawn, but we all ran. It was a night I will never forget!

It is beautiful to see the Bride of Messiah run after the Lord together. Corporate prayer is a good example of this. As the Bride of Messiah begins to seek the Lord with one heart and mind and *in one accord* as the scripture says, we will *all* receive the prize: an imperishable crown and *Yeshua* Himself. He is the greatest prize of all!

Get ready to run today — and remember to bring a friend along!

Day 14

King Solomon, *Shlomo HaMelech*, was anointed King of Israel (1 Kings 1:39). Anointing as a part of the coronation ceremony was done in obedience to a Divine command. The King was called *the Lord's anointed. Yeshua* is not only a King. He is the King of kings, in the same way that His song is The Song of Songs. His anointing far surpasses the anointing of Solomon or any earthly king. He is THE *Mashiach*, THE Anointed One of God.

In John 18:33-38, we read about Pilate questioning *Yeshua* concerning His kingship. *"Are You the King of the Jews?"* Pilate asked. *Yeshua* answered, *"My kingdom is not of this world..."* (verse 36) and *"You say rightly that I am a king. For this cause I was born, and for this cause I have come into the world..."* (verse 37).

Is *Yeshua* your King? Does He have complete lordship over your life? Or is He merely the One who saved you from your sin, the King of the Jews? For salvation to be all that God intended it to be, for your joy to be full, *Yeshua* must be King of your life. He is interested in every aspect of our lives and desires to be consulted *before* we make our plans. He is King and desires to rule supreme in our lives. This involves total submission from the heart to His divine will.

Yeshua is a King of Love. He is a Bridegroom King. The Jewish people of His time were expecting another type of king—a warrior-king like King David, one who would overthrow the Roman rule and set up His kingdom in power. But *Yeshua* came to usher in a different kind of kingdom—a kingdom of the heart. His reign more closely paralleled Solomon's than David's. Solomon's reign was a

28

reign of peace.

Yeshua's kingship brought peace also; however, this peace was on the inside, through redemption and reconciliation with the God of Abraham, Isaac, and Jacob. At His second coming, our Messiah King will come with the armies of Heaven and will strike the nations with a sharp sword that comes out of His mouth (Revelation 19:14-15). Until that day, we have special access to the gentle King of Love who extends a golden scepter to each member of His Bride as He answers the cry of our hearts and draws us into intimate communion with Himself.

At traditional Jewish weddings, the bridegroom is considered a "king," and his bride, his "queen." As the Bride of Messiah—a bride comprised of men, women, and children—we have a Bridegroom who is a King and who wants with all His heart to give us a kingdom of righteousness, peace, joy, and much more in the Spirit of God! But we must crown Him King—sovereign over our lives—before we can really know Him as the Bridegroom of our souls.

If *Yeshua* is our King, then He is our Lord. When He speaks, we must obey. There can be no such answer as "No, Lord," when *Yeshua* asks us to do something. He knows best. His ways are far higher than our ways. He loves us. He can be trusted. Is He telling you to do something today? Submission to His will and obedience to His commands are the pathway to joy in the Kingdom.

Bow your heart before *Yeshua* the King today. Call Him your "King" in prayer with love and reverence. Give honor and glory to the King of kings, the King of Glory, the King of the Jews. He wants to give you the Kingdom!

$\mathcal{D}ay\ 15$

The king hath brought me into his chambers.
Song of Songs 1:4

The Hebrew word for *chambers* is *cheder* (pronounced KHEH-der) and means *an apartment, bed, innermost part or chamber.* The chamber is a private place, a place of intimacy. The chambers spoken of in this verse represent the private dwelling place of God or *Yeshua.* The God of Abraham, Isaac, and Jacob brought the nation of Israel into His chambers once a year on the Day of Atonement, as the High Priest, who represented the people, went through the veil into the Holy of Holies bringing the blood of atonement with him. And during their time in the wilderness, God dwelt among His people in an intimate way, covering them with a cloud by day and warming them with His fire by night. He fed them from His table on high and gave them water from a rock that followed them.

Yeshua brings us into His chambers as we approach the throne of grace and worship Him *in spirit and in truth.* When He died on the tree, the huge veil in the Temple was torn in two, signifying that access to the Holy of Holies had been made available through the shed blood of the King of the Jews—24 hours a day, 365 days a year. *Yeshua* is in the holiest of places waiting for us. He desires our company far more than we desire His! He wants to be ALONE with us so that we can get to KNOW Him. He already knows us!

In 1980, when I was seven-years-old in the Lord, I began to study The Song of Songs. Up until that time I had a fairly strong devotional relationship with the Lord and was spending at least an hour a day alone with Him, sometimes at the piano with my Bible in front of me, at other times alone in my bedroom.

As the Lord began to draw me more and more into "The Song," my desire for time alone with God began to increase. My soul hungered and thirsted for more of the King. The five years that I spent in the chambers of the King, basking in His presence and delighting in His love, were the best years of my life. I would pray, then sing, sometimes dance before the Lord, worship, laugh, cry, read, then *listen*. I did a lot of listening.

Many times, Neil would knock at our bedroom door and find me on my knees with a bridal wreath on my head. He needed me in the ministry office (which at that time was in our home). I would say to him, "I'm just on introductions. I haven't started to pray yet." I'll never forget the look on his face as he said, "After two hours, you're still on introductions?" He was so good to allow me to stay in the King's chambers a while longer.

This is the place of ultimate peace, joy, and an unconditional love that cannot be put into words. And yet it's such a struggle for most of us to take time to be alone with our King! If you're single, or married without children, as I was for fourteen years, take advantage of the wonderful opportunity you have to spend uninterrupted time with the King in His chambers. Let Him love you, speak to you, touch you, and reveal Himself and His ways to you.

There is absolutely no substitute for getting alone with God. The "chamber experience" can be ours as we allow the *Ruach HaKodesh* (Holy Spirit) to draw us within the veil.

God is so Good,
God is so Loving,
God is so Real.
Press into His loving arms today,
in the chambers of the King.

Day 16

But thou, when thou prayest, enter into thy closet, and when thou hast shut thy door, pray to thy Father which is in secret...   Matthew 6:6

The believer's *closet*, mentioned here, is a type of *chamber or place of intimacy, a secret place of prayer,* where God, our Heavenly Father, gives His children a warm welcome. We shared this truth with a dear friend of ours who is a new Jewish believer in *Yeshua* after hearing that when she is very upset, she goes into a closet in her home and tells everything to her father whose ashes are in a box in that closet. She said that somehow she feels better after venting her frustration and anger, even though her father has been dead many years and can't hear her or do anything for her. We directed our friend to Matthew 6:6 and told her that she has a Father in Heaven who is alive and not only hears our prayers but answers the cry of our hearts!

What is your concept of God as Father? Do you see Him as loving, giving, and caring, or as harsh, uncaring, and punitive — or somewhere in between? We have found over the years that many people have a wrong concept of God the Father and that this is often based on their relationship with their earthly father.

A child who has been abused, neglected, or ridiculed by his or her father will generally have a difficult time seeing God as He really is: a God of love, mercy, tenderness, and kindness. This is an important truth for many adults: The God of the Bible is very different from the father you knew! Your Heavenly Father thinks you're wonderful and special and is interested in the details of your life.

"God is not a man, that He should lie, nor a son of man, that He should repent" (Numbers 23:19). This was a prophecy

given by Balaam in obedience to God. Balaam continued this prophecy by saying that he had received a command to bless, and when God blesses, it is irreversible.

I have the sense in my spirit today that God wants to bless you. He is the Father of blessings. The blessing He wants to impart is a deep revelation of the Fatherhood of God and His love for you, His child. Until you know the love of God as Father, you won't be able to fully comprehend the love of *Yeshua* as the Bridegroom of your soul.

Go into your room (*closet*). Shut the door. Pray to your Father in the secret place. Pour out your heart to Him. Renounce any spirit of rejection, deception, self-pity, and condemnation. Welcome and receive the love of your Heavenly Father, the Holy Spirit of God, the Spirit of Truth. He accepts you just the way you are. There's a secret He wants you to know: God, your Heavenly Father, is crazy about you!

Day 17

We will be glad and rejoice in thee.
Song of Songs 1:4

The first fruit of the chamber experience is JOY. Sometimes I wonder why so many believers lack joy. Could it be that Bible studies, prayer meetings, worship services, and other programs have replaced the basic foundation of the holiness walk: private time with the King?

The word *glad* in Hebrew is *giyl* (pronounced 'gheel'). It comes from a primary root that means *to spin around under the influence of any strong emotion.* This kind of gladness is not passive! The bride of Messiah should be dancing for joy over her union with the Beloved. "I am loved! He desires me! He has chosen me!" These are sentiments based on fact; they should take flight in joyful exclamations.

The Hebrew word for rejoice in this verse is *samach* (pronounced 'sah-mach') and means *to brighten up, cheer up, or be made merry.* Sometimes circumstances of life are such that we don't feel like rejoicing. This is where the "will" comes in. The word *will*, in fact, is found three times in verse four: *"we WILL run,"* *"we WILL be glad,"* and *"we WILL remember."* The Holy Scriptures exhort us to rejoice as an act of the will — in spite of external circumstances. To do this is a real act of faith and trust. God is pleased when we exercise our will and rejoice in Him when all else seems to be collapsing around us. He sees what we do not see and operates according to a spiritual reality that's far greater than the physical reality we tend to live in from day to day.

I remember rejoicing and praising the Lord as I held my father's hand and he breathed his last breath. It was an unlikely time to experience joy, but the reality of Heaven flooded my soul. I was so grateful that after years of resisting, Daddy was on his way home.

Joy is continually connected with the PRESENCE of GOD. One of my favorite verses is Psalm 16:11: *"...In Your presence is fullness of joy; at Your right hand are pleasures forevermore."* There will be *joy unspeakable, and full of glory* in Heaven, and there can be *fullness of joy* on earth, as well. *Yeshua* promised us that joy before He went to the cross. He said, in John 15:11, *"These things I have spoken to you, that My joy may remain in you, and that your joy may be full."* What things? *Yeshua* had just finished instructing His disciples to abide in His love. This was the secret of having *Yeshua*'s joy in their lives. How do we abide in His love?

Live in Him, move in Him, have your very being in Him, spend time in His presence, and let His Word burn deeply in your heart so that keeping His commandments becomes as natural as breathing.

Receive *Yeshua*'s love and joy will supernaturally follow.

Need a concrete place to begin?

Rejoice that your name is written in Heaven.

Day 18

We will remember thy love more than wine.
Song of Songs 1:4

Remembering God and all that He has done for His people is a theme that runs throughout Scripture. It's easy to forget the expressions of love we experienced last week, last month, or last year, when *today* is what really matters to us. "What has God done for me *today*?" is an attitude we're all guilty of adopting. And yet, if we look back to the evidence of the love in our lives we've been shown in the past, our present faith will be greatly strengthened and our hope renewed.

In the book of Exodus, God told His people to remember the day that He *brought them out of the house of bondage*. In Numbers, He told them to make fringes on the borders of their garments in order to *remember all the commandments of the Lord and do them*. In Deuteronomy, the Lord told His people to remember how He *led them all the way* during their forty years in the wilderness, fed them with manna, and kept their garments from wearing out. Then He urged them to remember that it is *God* who gives His people *power to get wealth*.

The last *remember* in the Old Testament Scriptures is found in Malachi 4:4 where the Lord of hosts exhorts His people to *"remember the law of Moses, My servant, which I commanded him in Horeb for all Israel, with the statutes and judgments..."*

Remembering God, His loving care, His Word, His marvelous works, and His provision for His people continues into the *Brit HaDasha* (New Covenant Scriptures) where the Messiah, *Yeshua*, connects remembering with His sacrifice for our sin. Referring to the cup of redemption and the unleavened Passover *matzah*, *Yeshua* said: *"This is*

My body which is given for you...This cup is the new covenant in My blood, which is shed for you. Do this in remembrance of Me" (from Luke 22:19-22).

Remember *Yeshua*. Remember His love. Remember His death and resurrection.

There was a time in our lives as believers when Neil and I experienced an onslaught of enemy attacks over a period of a few months. We felt a need to be strengthened daily and sought the Lord for direction. He led us to participate in the Lord's Supper (the *matzah* and fruit of the vine of the Passover *seder)* daily in our home, to remember His love and His victory at Calvary, and to appropriate it in our lives. This daily act of remembering *Yeshua* was a powerful spiritual weapon for us. We were able to triumph in Messiah by remembering Him.

Early in our walk with the Lord, we also discovered another way to remember God's love. We call them "miracle books." When God would speak to us from His Word, answer prayers, reveal a truth to us about ourselves or something in the Bible, or simply show us more about Himself, we would write it down in a little book. From time to time we would reread our miracle books to encourage ourselves in the Lord and build our faith. We would see all that God had done in the past, and realize that He's *the same yesterday, today, and forever,* and that His love never fails! Let us *forget not all His benefits* and remember His love as a daily spiritual exercise.

Why not begin today?

"I remember the day that *Yeshua* saved me…"

"I remember the time God healed me..."

"I remember the friend God sent to help me..."

"I remember..."

Day 19

The upright love thee.   Song of Songs 1:4

The Hebrew word for *upright* indicates *straightness and rectitude*. Rashi, a famous Jewish scholar, interprets *straightness* in this verse as a modifying noun: *"the sincerity of their love for You — a strong love, straight and void of deceit or roughness."* Therefore, we could rephrase the text to read: "Sincerely do they love thee."

What is sincere love for God? Have you ever been in a worship service where the entire congregation sang words such as *"Nothing I desire compares with You"* and *"You are all I need"?* Did it make you feel uncomfortable? Sometimes I feel convicted listening to myself sing such choruses to God. Do I really mean what I am singing? I stop to think about it and ask the Holy Spirit to search my heart.

The heart is deceitful above all things, and desperately wicked (Jeremiah 17:9). We really don't know our own hearts. It's very easy to go around telling people how much we love God, but the truth of the matter is that our love for Him will show by what we do, whether we proclaim it verbally or not.

The Holy Scriptures tell us that sincere love always culminates in action. *Yeshua* expressed it as follows, in John 14:15 and 21: *"If you love Me, keep My commandments. He who has My commandments and keeps them, it is he who loves Me. And he who loves Me will be loved by My Father, and I will love him and manifest Myself to him."*

Sincere love for God compels us to live according to His Word. It is mixed with a godly fear that keeps us teachable — and open to correction by others, as well as by the Holy Spirit.

The word *sincere* comes from two Latin words: *sine* and

38

cere, which mean *without wax*. In ancient times, a potter would often put his seal or stamp upon a completed vessel with the words *sine cere*. This meant that to his knowledge there was no flaw in that work. If a potter did crack a vessel, he would carefully patch that flawed vase or bowl by filling in the crack with wax. Then he would glaze it over. But it did not merit the stamp *sine cere* (without wax) because it was not a flawless piece of pottery.

Perhaps your love of God has not been without flaw. Repent, and ask the Father to help you love Him in sincerity and in truth. God is calling His children to greater transparency in these last days. Sin hides; it seeks dark places. Truth and sincerity come to the light. They have nothing to hide. And in the light, there is fellowship with God as well as with our family members and our brothers and sisters in the Lord.

We would do well to heed the words that the Lord God of Israel spoke through Joshua, before his death, to all the tribes of Israel: *"Now therefore, fear the LORD, serve Him in sincerity and in truth, and put away the gods which your fathers served on the other side of the River and in Egypt. Serve the Lord!"* (Joshua 24:14).

Pray with me:

> *Heavenly Father, I want to love You in sincerity and in truth. I want my life to be "without wax," without hidden defects, so that Satan does not have a foothold or a point of entrance. Help me to yield to Your Spirit as You mold me and make me into a vessel for Your glory. Please hold me tight in the firing process.*
>
> > *In Yeshua's name,*
> > *Amen*

$\mathcal{D}ay$ 20

I am black, but comely... as the tents of Kedar, as the curtains of Solomon.   Song of Songs 1:5

This is the bride's confession following the "chamber experience." Isaiah had a similar experience, as recorded in Isaiah 6:1-5: *"In the year that King Uzziah died, I saw the Lord sitting on a throne, high and lifted up, and the train of His robe filled the temple"* (verse 1). *"So I said: 'Woe is me, for I am undone! Because I am a man of unclean lips, and I dwell in the midst of a people of unclean lips; for my eyes have seen the King, the Lord of Hosts'"* (verse 5).

When we are drawn into the presence of the King, we behold His glory, His purity, His power, and sense the bold contrast between who He is and who we are! *"I am black [dark], but comely"* is a realistic assessment of who the Bride of Messiah really is. Blackness (darkness) here represents the self-life, the unrenewed mind, that part of us that was crucified and buried with Messiah. As we grow in *Yeshua*, there should be less and less evidence of any "darkness" in us.

God shows us a pattern of going from dark to light in creation. We read in the book of Genesis that the day begins in the evening, at dark. It is not God's way to end in darkness. He brings us from darkness to light. We have a future that is brighter than our present! But right now, no matter how much darkness there may be in our lives, the Bridegroom sees us as *comely*—beautiful, forgiven, new creations with a new nature. While it's true that we're not perfect yet, we are in the process of becoming. We need to agree with our adversary (Satan) quickly in this regard, and then move on. He tries to get us to focus on all our shortcomings. But the Scripture makes it clear that *in Yeshua*, we are complete. We are *accepted in the Beloved*!

This verse is an excellent example of Hebrew parallelism. *"Black as the tents of Kedar"* is contrasted with *"comely as the curtains of Solomon."* *Kedar* refers to a tribe of nomads descended from Ishmael who lived in tents made of black goatskin (Genesis 25:13, Psalms 120:5). They were a warlike people. This is in sharp contrast to *Solomon* who represents *peace*. *The curtains of Solomon* that adorned the Tabernacle were of blue and purple and crimson and fine white linen with cherubim woven into them — not at all like a goatskin tent.

Verse five is a study in contrasts. On one level the Shulamite maiden, as a lower class field worker, is browned by extended exposure to the sun. The daughters of Jerusalem, whom she addresses, are pale, pampered ladies of the court. In those days, it was not at all fashionable to get a suntan. The Shulamite tries to get *the daughters* to look beyond her outward blackness to her inward beauty.

Our inward beauty is not ours; it is the Lord's, for in *us* dwells *no good thing*. However, we have been washed, cleansed, made new through the blood of the Lamb.

We are *comely* in the Messiah. He sees us through eyes of love. He sees us *in Him* and He sees us as we shall be. He sees the white, blue, and scarlet of the curtains in us. The white speaks of righteousness and sins forgiven, the blue of the divine nature imparted to us in *Yeshua*, the red of His blood that has cleansed us of all sin, and the purple of His majesty and our calling as a holy priesthood. Let our confession be today: *"I am black, but comely."* None of us is perfect yet. We are all in the process of becoming. Humility, coupled with assurance of our position in Messiah, is the attitude most becoming *Yeshua's* Bride.

$\mathcal{D}ay\ 21$

The *daughters of Jerusalem* play a supporting role in The Song of Songs. Their identity has been speculated upon for centuries by Jewish and Christian scholars alike. According to many Orthodox Jewish expositors, the *daughters of Jerusalem* represent the *goyim*, the nations of the world, since the day will come when people from all countries will come up to Jerusalem. Thus, in a poetical sense, they are her *daughters.*

If we follow this line of reasoning, then Israel would be the one who says: *"I am black, but comely."* Truly, the heart of God longs for that day when Israel recognizes her spiritual blackness. It is difficult for a people who have suffered so much at the hands of "Christians" and have made such great humanitarian, scientific, and literary contributions to the world to see themselves as "sinners." Contrast with a Holy God, as opposed to one's fellow man, makes this more comprehensible. Pray for the Jewish people. Their redemption is only a prayer away, and with it the deepest fulfillment and completion that a Jewish person could ever have.

Many traditional Christian commentaries define *the daughters* as *those who are close to the Kingdom, but not in it.* They are not *the virgins.* They are not *the Bride.* They very well might represent the same group *Yeshua* referred to in Luke 23:28, a people related to God through covenant: *"Daughters of Jerusalem, do not weep for Me, but weep for ourselves and for your children."*

These daughters could represent the inhabitants of the city of Jerusalem or, in a larger sense, the entire Jewish people. The bride is just beginning to dialogue with them. She wants the Jewish people to see the King's beauty, not her blackness. The Bride of Messiah has been called *from the foundation of the world* to provoke the Jew to jealousy. Sadly, for the most part, she has thus far just managed to provoke the Jew.

As true believers in *Yeshua HaMashiach* begin to walk in love and humility, sincerity and truth before the Jewish people, there will be meaningful dialogue. Jewish people are hungry today. They are looking for spiritual reality. Pray that they might see the beauty of the Messiah in you. Pray *for the peace of Jerusalem*! Intercede for *the daughters of Jerusalem*. Remember that to them belong *the adoption, the glory, the covenants, the giving of the law, the service of God, and the promises* (Romans 9:4).

God is not through with the Jewish people! On the contrary, today is the day that He is drawing them by His Spirit and revealing their Messiah to them. In the same way that the Lord God breathed life into man in the Garden of Eden (a kiss?), He is kissing the Jewish people today, and new creations in Messiah are coming forth. If you've never shared *Yeshua* with a Jewish person, ask God to give you the opportunity. You have been *called to the Kingdom for such a time as this*! You have a special treasure to share with *the daughters of Jerusalem*: *Yeshua*, the most precious Jewish jewel of all!

Day 22

*Look not upon me, because I am black,
because the sun hath looked upon me.*
Song of Songs 1:6

No one likes to have his/her sin exposed. Hiding sin is a natural thing to do. We see it at the very beginning of time in the Garden of Eden. The Bible tells us that Adam and Eve hid themselves from the presence of the Lord God after they had eaten of the forbidden fruit (Genesis 3:8).

Allowing our sin to be exposed, not insisting that the self-life be dealt with in secret, being honest and transparent before God and others is a work of supernatural grace. It is also great wisdom. If we can share our areas of temptation and sins with someone else, we not only enlist prayer support but expose darkness in such a way that its hold on us is loosened. We are instructed, in James 5:16, to *"confess [your] faults one to another, and pray one for one another, that ye may be healed" (KJV).*

We tend to be quick to give reasons for our blackness, even as the Shulamite gave her explanation about the sun. We justify and rationalize. I just realized that (coincidentally) I've been sitting out here in my backyard writing for almost four hours. The Florida sun is turning my skin a brown color. Yes, I'm using sunscreen; however, I probably should be inside instead of out here. But it feels so nice in the sun, and my hair will get a shade lighter if I stay out here all day! We have reasons for everything we do. Then if things go wrong, we tend to place the blame on someone else, many times on God Himself. But no one makes us sin. We *choose* to expose ourselves to the sun: violence, profanity, or ungodliness in many forms.

"Forgive me, Father. I have sinned" are sweet words

44

to the heart and ears of our God. Repentance restores our relationship with the Lord and sets us free. Never forget the wonderful promise of forgiveness found in 1 John 1:9: *"If we confess our sins, He is faithful and just to forgive us our sins and to cleanse us from all unrighteousness."*

Daily repentance is a must for the Bride of Messiah. Without it, we block the flow of God's love in our lives. *Yeshua* delights in forgiving our sin. He died for us *"while we were still sinners"* (Romans 5:8).

The King of Israel, Solomon, loved the Shulamite field worker even in her darkened condition. In the same way, *Yeshua* loved us while we were steeped in sin. He sought us out in the highways of life. Knowing our shortcomings and all our faults, He loves us still. What a miracle! His grace is *greater than all our sin.*

Have you sinned? Confess it, forsake it, and go on with God!

Perhaps, like a friend of mine, you were sinned against as a child. Debbie was sexually abused by both her parents. There were no boundaries in her very dysfunctional household, and she grew up feeling violated and dirty. When Debbie received *Yeshua* as her Messiah, a healing process began, and she was able to bring her past darkness into the light. Today, she is a beautiful part of the Bride of Messiah.

Whether our spiritual darkness is the result of our sin or the sins of others, the solution is the same: the cleansing work of God. I'm so thankful for the wonderful truth expressed in 1 John 1:7: *"...the blood of Yeshua HaMashiach His [God's] Son cleanses us from all sin."*

Day 23

My mother's children were angry with me;
they made me the keeper of the vineyards.
Song of Songs 1:6

It's always easier to blame others rather than to take the blame ourselves. This is particularly evident in the basic building block of the Body of believers—the home. The family is late for services, no one has clean socks, the dog got out, the milk carton is empty. Someone else is to blame. This pattern of behavior began in the very first family, with Adam.

When God asked Adam if he had eaten from the tree of which He commanded him not to eat, Adam replied, *"The woman whom You gave to be with me, she gave me of the tree, and I ate"* (Genesis 3:12). Adam placed the blame on Eve. He took no responsibility for his own actions. In the same way, wives blame husbands, children blame their parents and each other, and on it goes, as we rationalize and are unwilling to accept responsibility and be accountable. In the same way, the Shulamite blames her mother's children for her own condition.

What mother is the Shulamite maiden referring to here? The one who gave birth to her could be called "the Church," "the Body," or the "system of grace" in a global sense. The mother's children would then be other believers, or members of the same spiritual family. Unfortunately, just as we blame others within our natural families, believers are often quick to blame their brothers and sisters in the Lord, especially those in leadership positions. The pastor or rabbi is often the one who is "wrong."

The "bridal-soul" seems to be saying in this verse that she has been made to do something against her will. Perhaps

46

she was strongly encouraged to be a Sunday school teacher or a nursery attendant, or to be a worker in the Body of Messiah. Maybe she was admonished to "get involved." Doing what others want instead of seeking the Lord's guidance and doing His will leads to resentment. We have no one to blame but ourselves when we go beyond what God has asked us to do. Pointing the finger at someone else is not pleasing to our Father.

The Lord spoke some words through the prophet Isaiah, in chapter 58:9-11, which tells us what God will do for us when we obey Him: *"If you take away the yoke from your midst, the pointing of the finger, and speaking wickedness ...you shall be like a watered garden..."*

A watered garden, a beautiful vineyard, will characterize us as we learn to say, "It was my fault," "I am sorry," "Please forgive me," and "I was wrong." These are all healthy, spiritually elevating phrases that come from the lips of a humble soul who is committed to doing the will of God. To such a person *Yeshua* gives bountiful grace.

Does that include you? It can!

Pray with me:

"Search me, O God, and know my heart; try me, and know my anxieties; and see if there is any wicked way in me, and lead me in the way everlasting" (Psalm 139:23-24). Help me to accept responsibility for my actions and to say, 'I am sorry. Please forgive me. I was wrong,' as You give me the grace to humble myself."

Day 24

But mine own vineyard have I not kept.
Song of Songs 1:6

This part of verse six has always had a powerfully convicting effect on me personally. So many times I have let the Lord down, ignored Him, grieved His heart, made Him sad, by neglecting my own vineyard—my personal relationship with Him. This is an area of potential danger, especially for those who serve the Lord in a full-time capacity. We tend to be so busy "keeping the vineyards" that our own vineyard has a low priority. This is sin!

Proverbs 24:30-34 addresses this spiritual problem: *"I went by the field of the slothful, and by the vineyard of the man [or woman] devoid of understanding; and there it was, all overgrown with thorns; its surface was covered with nettles, its stone wall was broken down. When I saw it, I considered it well; I looked on it and received instruction: a little sleep, a little slumber, a little folding of the hands to rest; so your poverty will come like a prowler, and your want like an armed man."*

When we are slothful with our own vineyard, spiritual poverty is the result. We are God's garden. Our greatest "work" is to get to know Him. And that happens when we keep our own vineyard free from weeds (through confession of sin), well-watered (through time in the Word and in prayer), with our wall up and strong (through putting on the full armor of God on a daily basis).

I've spent more time than usual lately out in our yard. The hedge along our fence was just about dead, so we replanted it with new ficus plants. They had to be watered daily for two weeks in order to get a good start. I told Neil that I would be faithful to water the plants. I have been, but God has been even more faithful. He has sent water from Heaven at least every other day since the hedge was planted. I learned a lesson from this. If we're just "willing," God will meet us more than halfway!

Yesterday we had to replace my favorite tree which stood in front of the house. Our rabbi had given it to us as a Hanukkah present. It's called a Tibouchina, or "purple glory tree." I had spent a year and a half fertilizing it, caring for it, praying over it, and greatly enjoying it as it flourished and grew. Then suddenly, it began to die. I noticed some marks on the bark of the trunk, where the lawn man's weed whacker had obviously lashed into the tree. Within a few weeks, the glory tree was dead. We called many nurseries in the area trying to find another tree (they come from California), and we finally located one. It was the exact same size as the one that died. We planted it yesterday, and it is as if we've had a resurrection from the dead. The lawn service agreed to pay for it, and we're expecting the glory of the second tree to exceed the glory of the former.

God is a God of restoration who can make all things new! Tend your vineyard. God will provide the water for you. He will send showers of blessings. And *the latter glory* (fruit) of your relationship with *Yeshua* will be greater than anything you've known in the past. The best is yet to come!

P.S. But expect a battle. The second "purple glory tree" succumbed to the weed whacker too. Again the lawn service paid for a new tree. This one was more glorious than the first two (*"from glory to glory"*). We finally caught on and planted a little wall around tree number three.

P.P.S. I couldn't believe my eyes! The other day I discovered that the weed whacker had been used *inside* the cement wall. There may yet be a "glory tree" number 4!

Day 25

Thou hast brought a vine out of Egypt...
Psalm 80:8

The vine or *vineyard,* as a metaphor, is found throughout the Holy Scriptures. A study of some of these references helps us understand more clearly God's plan for the Shulamite's (our) vineyard.

God brought a people out of Egypt and made them a nation at Mount Sinai when He gave them His Law (their marriage contract). He chose the Jewish people as His wife; she was to be a fruitful vine at His table. God planted His vine, prepared room for it, and caused it to take deep root, and it filled the land that God had promised to His people (Psalm 80:8-9).

We also read about God's vine (actually called His *"vineyard"*) in the book of Isaiah chapter five in a *mashal,* or type of Hebrew parable. The Lord expected His vine to bring forth good grapes, but instead, it brought forth wild grapes (bad fruit). God's judgment on His vineyard, called *"the house of Israel"* in verse seven, is harsh indeed: *"I will take away its hedge, and it shall be burned; and break down its wall, and it shall be trampled down. I will lay it waste; it shall not be pruned or dug, but there shall come up briers and thorns. I will also command the clouds that they rain no rain on it"* (Isaiah 5:5-6).

We read in the *Brit Hadasha,* in John chapter 15, that the judgment on anyone who does not abide in *"the Vine"* (*Yeshua*) is being cast out as a branch, and being thrown into the fire and burned (John 15:6). We also read, in Matthew 3:10, of a similar fate for those who do not bear good fruit: *"Therefore every tree which does not bear good fruit is cut down and thrown into the fire."*

The vines that God plants are meant to produce good fruit. What happened to Israel? What happens to us when we are not fruitful?

One of the things that happens is that the vine that God brought out of spiritual Egypt becomes captive again — in bondage to lies, fears, doubts, the cares and deceptions of this world.

As we continue in Isaiah five, the prophet says, *"Therefore my people have gone into captivity, because they have no knowledge..."* (Isaiah 5:13). Ignorant of who God really is and what His Word says about how we are to live, we end up calling evil good and good evil. We become wise in our own eyes. We are valiant at mixing intoxicating drink. We take away justice from the righteous man (Isaiah 5:20-23). This is precisely what has happened in our once "Christian country" and is in danger of happening in the Body of believers as well.

Some (but not all) of Israel has gone into captivity by rejecting the Law of the Lord and despising the Word of the Holy One of Israel. Some (but not all) of the Church is in bondage because it has decided what part of the Bible to accept and has discarded the rest. This is not good fruit.

Good fruit grows as believers abide in *Yeshua*, the True Vine, and walk in His truth. The truth sets us free. The people God brought out of Egypt were alive, and they were free. They were redeemed by the blood of the lamb. Messiah's Bride is called to be a fruitful vine, alive, free, and redeemed by the blood of the Lamb.

Lord, help us to fulfill our calling to bear fruit. Thank You for new life in Yeshua, the True Vine. Cause me to cling to Him, to abide in Him forevermore. Amen

$\mathscr{D}$ay 26

Tell me, O thou whom my soul loveth ...
Song of Songs 1:7

Soul in Hebrew is *nephesh*, a word that literally means *a breathing creature* and comes from the primary root *to breathe*. This noun refers to *the essence of life, the act of breathing*, and might be translated *inner self* in English.

The word for *love* in this verse is *ahavah*, the same word used in Deuteronomy to express a parallel idea about a soul that loves: *"Hear, O Israel: The Lord our God, the Lord is one! You shall love the Lord your God with all your heart, with all your SOUL, and with all your might"* (Deuteronomy 6:4-5).

This kind of love for God is the kind that martyrs throughout the years (both Jewish and Christian) have exemplified. With their last breath, they have given glory to God. They have demonstrated what it is to love God with all their soul. Whether Jewish or not, they have personified the "Jewish heart" that God longs to find in His children.

Neil often quotes a story from *Faithful Unto Death*, a book about fifteen young people who were not afraid to die for their faith. This story made a lasting impact on his walk with the Lord. It still speaks to us about what it means to love God with one's whole soul.

Joost Joosten, an 18-year-old Anabaptist who lived in the southwest Netherlands in the sixteenth century, came to understand faith as a personal trust in Messiah rather than a creedal ascent to Christian doctrine, at a time when it was against the law to believe this way. He was arrested shortly after his eighteenth birthday, imprisoned, and tortured in an effort to turn him from his faith. Various methods of torture were used, such as stretching his body on a rack, but Joost would not yield.

Finally, after other methods of torture were unsuccessful, the inquisitors developed a new procedure which they were certain would break his will. The instrument of torture was called an "iron *teerlingen.*" With Joost seated on a chair, the jailors would thrust long thin pointed rods of iron in at his knees and by turning and pressing drive them through his lower legs until they came out at his ankles. Even the men who administered the torture were shaken by his suffering and the spirit and faith with which he resisted them.

Joost could not be forced to surrender. His faith in Jesus only grew stronger, so a sentence was passed that he was to be put to death by burning. Joost was brought from the prison to the straw hut where he was to die. In spite of the pain of walking on his bruised legs, he sang joyously. When he came to the area for the execution, he gave witness to his faith in Messiah and the cause for which he died. Joost lifted his voice and sang his favorite composition, *"O Lord, you are forever in my thoughts."* Then he walked into the little straw hut.

Deep, willing-to-sacrifice love for the Lord is not generated by the mind, and cannot be manufactured by any of us. It is rooted in the Spirit of the Lord who floods the soul with this supernatural love in much the same way that love is imparted to a mother's soul when she sees her newborn child for the first time. But there is one big difference. The newborn hasn't done anything to merit such love, while God has.

How has He loved us? *Let me count the ways!* The Father loved us enough to send His only Son to die in our place. The Son loved us enough to come. Then He loved us too much to leave us comfortless, so He left us His Spirit to make sure that He would still be present with us. And now *Yeshua* loves us daily by interceding for us at the right hand of the Father.

There's nothing greater in this world than the love of God! This love is what the soul longs for. We were created to share in the love of God. Our souls find fulfillment in the Beloved (Jesus) and nourishment in His Word.

The Bible is God's love letter to your soul. Approach it in that manner, and allow your soul to breathe in a bit of Heaven. The soul, *nephesh,* that is loved greatly should greatly love.

But if you don't love the Lord greatly and would like to, follow the advice of a little girl who discovered a sacred secret. She repeated to herself, *"Yeshua* (Jesus) loves me," over and over again. "It was through Him that the flowers, the birds, and everything beautiful were created. He went through a lifetime of suffering and died on the cross in great sorrow, for me. He offers me forgiveness for all my sins and a life full of joy. He loves me, for sure." *

Before you know it, without trying, you too will love Him.

* *(From the book, **From The Lips of Children**, by Richard Wurmbrand)*

Day 27

*...it [is] the blood [that] maketh an atonement for
the soul.* Leviticus 17:11

The principles of God are unchanging. It has always been
God's way to bring deliverance and freedom through blood.
The Exodus from Egypt is a good example of this. The
Israelites were instructed to apply the blood of an innocent
lamb, by faith, so that the angel of death would pass over
them. When the Jews had a tabernacle, the High Priest
brought blood into the Holy of Holies to make atonement
for the sins of God's people. Always blood. Today in
Jerusalem they have even recreated the silver receptacle
used for catching the blood of sacrifices in preparation for
the construction of the Third Temple.

What about the blood of Messiah? *Yeshua*, our Passover,
and the Lamb spoken of by the prophet Isaiah in chapter 53,
was led *like a sheep to the slaughter* and voluntarily laid down
His life for each one of us. His last words on the cross, *"It
is finished,"* have bridal overtones. The Hebrew word for
bride is *kallah* and comes from the primary root *kalal*, which
means *to complete, make perfect, or finish*. As His blood spilled
to the ground, *Yeshua's* last thought was of you — and me —
the joy that was set before Him — the reason He endured the
pain and despised the shame: His Bride! What love!

I like to think of the blood as not only the price paid for
my redemption, but the "bridal token" of my "newness" in
Yeshua — my status as a *"chaste virgin"* in Him, spoken of by
the Apostle Paul in 2 Corinthians 11:2. At the time of *Yeshua*,
Jewish brides often saved the sheets from their wedding
night, stained with blood, to prove that they were indeed
virgins when they married. In the same way, the blood of *Yeshua* proves that *we* are virgins. Truly His blood is precious!

In the early years of my walk with *Yeshua*, I spent many hours before Him, always with paper and pen in hand. I expected Him to speak to me, and He usually did. The Lord seemed to enjoy my childlikeness, and spoke to me in very concrete ways. On September 18, 1976, He dictated the following note to me. I pray that it touches your heart today.

"Fear not, for I am with thee. What I have put in your heart, *I* have put there. You do wrong to even wonder what the world or people might think, or be, or do. I require total obedience from you. My love for you knows no limits. You have accepted my Son, Jesus, and His blood is precious to you. Think how precious it must be to Me. You know the power in it, but you haven't seen it yet. You will."

Through the blood of our Bridegroom/King (God's Passover Lamb), we are at one with God. Through His blood, our souls are cleansed, redeemed, sanctified, and reconciled to God. God sees *you* through the blood of His Son! The blood speaks of life and forgiveness, mercy and cleansing. What a gift to be thankful for!

In *Yeshua*'s day, brides were purchased. As the bride of Messiah, we also have been bought with a price (1 Peter 1:18-19): the precious blood of Messiah, *as of a lamb without blemish or spot.* He loved us so much that He was willing to pay the supreme price for His bride—His life. When something is purchased at a great price, it means that item has great value.

You are of great value to God, and the blood proves it!

Day 28

... where thou feedest, where thou makest thy flock to rest at noon... Song of Songs 1:7

The Shulamite is asking her beloved a question here. *Where do you feed and make your flock to rest at noon?* She is addressing him as a shepherd who cares for his flock.

Does God want to answer our questions? Yes, He does! *"For everyone who asks receives, and he who seeks finds, and to him who knocks it will be opened"* (Matthew 7:8). The maiden's question is certainly in the will of God. She wants to know where she can go to find rest and refreshment. She desires spiritual nourishment. The Shulamite, at this point, is like many young believers who "just don't understand" yet. They do not yet know the ways of God.

It reminds me of our son Jonathan when he was two and a half years old. Neil rented a video for him from the video store. Jonathan asked him if he could keep the movie and Neil explained about "renting." At the same time, Neil also bought Jonathan a lollipop to have after dinner as a special treat. Jonathan was very concerned as they left the video store and asked, "Daddy, did you rent the lollipop, too?"

We learn some things as we grow! Rest and refreshment are found naturally as we follow the Messiah. It is the desire of the heart of God to provide nourishment for His children — even sweets at times. And the lollipops aren't rented! When God gives something to us, it is ours to keep. *Yeshua,* our Shepherd, longs to lead us beside still, sweet waters.

I just looked at the clock. It's 11:50 A.M. — almost noon, and the Lord just said to me, "Where you are, *I am!*" As I nibble on a graham cracker, the God of the whole universe is right here with me, because His Spirit dwells inside of me.

God wants to speak to us at noon. Daniel and other Old Covenant saints knew this secret. They prayed three times each day: in the morning, at noon, and in the evening. Noon is the hottest time of the day. In our country, it is usually lunchtime. Why not make noon a time for feeding your spirit as well? Read a portion from the Bread of Life; take a few moments to get alone with God and pray. Let God be your refuge from the fierce noonday sun. Where He is, there are green pastures, still waters, and a table prepared, even *in the presence of [your] enemies.*

Notice that the Shepherd spoken of in this verse *makes* His flock rest at noon in the same way that the Shepherd spoken of in Psalm 23 *makes* His flock *lie down in green pastures.* (This is also repeated in Ezekiel 34:15.) Shepherds know what is best for their sheep. Sheep need to rest during the hottest part of the day. But when we, as God's flock, experience the "high noon" of affliction, a time of distress, trouble, or tribulation, the last thing we usually want to do is rest. The natural response is to search frantically for a way out. But our Shepherd says the opposite: *"Be still!"*

Ask the Lord to help you to yield to His Spirit at noontime and at all times when the heat gets turned up spiritually. Labor to enter His rest. Your Shepherd has special treats in store for you.

Day 29

The Lord is my shepherd; I shall not want.

Psalm 23:1

The shepherd referred to in our last verse, Song 1:7, can be seen as the God of Israel, as well as His Messiah. God is portrayed as a Shepherd throughout the *Tanach*. Perhaps no verse of the Bible is as well known as Psalm 23:1. The One who created us and loves us is like a shepherd with his sheep. In Psalm 80, we read about God as *"the Shepherd of Israel."* In Isaiah 40:11, the prophet speaks of the God of Israel in these beautiful and gentle words: *"He will feed His flock like a shepherd; He will gather the lambs with His arm, and carry them in His bosom, and gently lead those who are with young."*

This is one of my favorite verses in the Bible, and one which I claimed for myself as a mother with young children. I have also shared it with many expectant mothers.

How we need a Shepherd to guide us! While the Bible calls God *the Shepherd of Israel*, *Yeshua* is called *The Good Shepherd*. We read, in Mark 6:34, that when He saw a great multitude, the Messiah was moved with compassion for them because they were *like sheep not having a shepherd*. So He began to teach them many things. Good teaching always comes from a "Shepherd heart" like that of *Yeshua*.

Did you notice that the beloved in The Song of Songs suddenly switched from being a King to being a Shepherd? This has caused much confusion and controversy over the centuries. So much so, that finally a Jewish commentary was written which concluded that there are two male protagonists in The Song: a king and a shepherd. According to this interpretation, the real lover of the Shulamite is the shepherd. The king tries to steal her affections, but she

59

longs for the shepherd, and finally is united with him.

This viewpoint cannot reconcile the king and shepherd being *one*. And yet, we have the example of King David who was both a shepherd and a king. *Yeshua*, in like manner, is both *the Good Shepherd* who gives His life for the sheep and *the King of the Jews*. But in the greater sense, when we apply the title Shepherd/King to *Yeshua*, we refer to His first coming as a Shepherd of love to usher in a kingdom of the heart, and His second coming as King of kings and Lord of lords, to usher in the Kingdom of God on earth, where His Kingship will be recognized by all.

Our Shepherd, the Lord *Yeshua*, owns us and is devoted to us. He is a *good* Shepherd. He is kind, gentle, intelligent, brave, and selfless. We are very much like sheep, often fearful, stubborn, even stupid, going along with the crowd, and yet our Shepherd chose us, bought us, calls us by name, and is always working on our behalf.

Our ministry began with a chorus, *"Love Song to the Messiah,"* that expresses my feelings for the Good Shepherd:

> *You are my Shepherd, my loving guide.*
> *You are the Rock in which I hide.*
> *You are my song in the daytime*
> *And my peaceful rest at night.*
> *You are my portion, and my delight!*

God wants to be all this and more to *you*! You are His, He is good, and He has a good plan for your life.

Day 30

Why should I be as one that turneth
aside by the flocks of thy companions?
Song of Songs 1:7

This portion of verse 7 could also be translated, "Why should I be like one veiled in mourning among the flocks of Your fellow shepherds?" or "Why must I stumble about in constant quest, bewildered?"

I can hear the Messiah answering, "You shouldn't. There's no reason to stumble. If you've been with Me all morning, you'll certainly know where I am at noon!" There's no reason to be "lost" in the Lord, for we have been found. We must cleave to Him even as He cleaves to us, from morning to night, from the beginning of our walk with *Yeshua* until He comes to take us home. Learning to lean on the Lord, to depend on Him, rather than on our own abilities and intelligence, is an important lesson to be learned. Leaning on *Yeshua* keeps us close to Him. Sometimes we're too strong, and this gets in the way of our leaning.

I'll never forget the time I was very sick in bed for a couple of weeks. I was extremely frustrated because I couldn't *do* anything. I was complaining to the Lord, telling Him that I was very weak and all my strength was gone when I heard a voice say, "Good! Perhaps now you can begin to live in *My* strength, not yours!"

At some point we must die to ourselves, our strengths, and our ideas, so *Yeshua* can live through us. The Apostle Paul set an example for us when he said, *"For when I am weak, then I am strong"* (2 Corinthians 12:10).

God gives us direction and strength to go on when we *acknowledge Him in all [our] ways.* While teaching preschool in a private school in Fort Lauderdale a few years after coming to know the Messiah, I learned another lesson about staying close to and depending on God. I had been assigned the "science" area in the preschool, and was given the task of developing the curriculum. This was very exciting and challenging to me. I love to develop curriculum. I enjoy science, and had lots of good creative ideas gathered from my Masters Degree work in Early Childhood Education. As I pondered how this assignment would be an easy one for me, I was stopped in my tracks by a still small voice in my head (or was it my heart?) that said, "You think you're so smart! You don't know anything. Why don't you let Me give you your ideas? Then you'll see what creativity really is!"

It seems to me that this happened around noon, right in the middle of the classroom, as the children were outside playing. From that moment on, I began to depend on God for my ideas in teaching. What joy! What great, exciting lesson plans He gave me!

You'll find God when you become like a child, trust His Words, and believe Him. Depend on His strength and you won't stumble. Your Shepherd wants to speak directly to you today!

Day 31

If thou know not, O thou fairest among women,
go thy way forth by the footsteps of the flock,
and feed thy kids beside the shepherds' tents.
Song of Songs 1:8

Have you noticed that although it is His song, the Shulamite has done all of the talking thus far? How like a new believer she is. When we first meet the Messiah, we also do more talking than listening.

Now, it is the Bridegroom's turn to speak. He addresses the Shulamite in adoring terms, calling her the *"fairest among women,"* and gives her specific guidance and direction. He shows her the way. He is the way! Proverbs 3:5-6 speaks of God's direction: *"Trust in the Lord with all your heart, and lean not on your own understanding; In all your ways acknowledge Him, and He shall direct your paths."* These verses have been words of life to me since July 25, 1973, when my mother inscribed them on the front page of a Bible she gave me as a going-away gift (not realizing that on that very same day I prayed to receive Jesus as my personal Savior and Lord).

If we ask Him, *Yeshua* WILL show us the way. He will direct us to others who are part of His flock who know Him intimately and can teach us His ways. The Lord is found in the midst of His people. We have the promise from Scripture that where two or more are gathered in His name, He is there in their midst (Matthew 18:20).

Gathering together with other believers, *not forsaking the assembling together* of those of like faith, is important for all of us, but particularly for those who are young in the Lord. God has placed under-shepherds in His Body to feed His sheep (because they love Him). Most of them serve in tents called churches or Messianic synagogues. It is His desire for individual believers to be committed to a local *tent*. Each of us as sheep not only has much to learn, but also much to give. Our individual talents and gifts were given for the edification of the flock. Lone rangers who choose not to submit to a local body or wandering Jews who go from tent to tent never experience the full blessing that God desires them to have. They miss out, and so do their "kids!"

There is no such place as a perfect *tent* (church, temple, fellowship), but there is a place where God wants each of us to serve, to learn, to grow, and to worship. If we ask Him to direct us there, He will show us the way. When we find the place God wants us to be, there is a special sense of peace and well-being that settles into our spirit, not because the shepherd is perfect, not because the flock is without problems, but because we are in the perfect will of God.

This has been our experience since 1973, first in a church for three years, then in the Messianic synagogue we began in Fort Lauderdale, Florida. Fed until we were spiritually overstuffed for three years, we came to understand that it was time for us to feed others. Very few believers in America are underfed or undernourished. God has given us all abundant spiritual food. It is time for most of us to begin feeding others!

Have you been joined to a local flock? Are your gifts and talents being used to build the Kingdom of God? This is not the hour to wander aimlessly. God wants to *establish* and *use* you while it is yet day. *"In all your ways acknowledge Him, and He shall direct your paths!"*

$\mathcal{D}ay$ 32

*I have compared thee, O my love, to
a company of horses in Pharaoh's chariots.*
Song of Songs 1:9

I brushed a horse this morning (a rare treat for me) at the
Kauffman barn in Bird-in-Hand, Pennsylvania. Surrounding
the barn are beautiful Amish farmlands. Horses hitched to
buggies periodically come down the lane, making striking
silhouettes against the lush fields of corn.

The horse is one of the most beautiful creatures that God
created. When our Heavenly Bridegroom compares us to a
horse, He is paying us a great compliment.

The Bible tells us that Solomon had forty thousand stalls
of horses for his chariots (1 Kings 4:26). He is said to have
gotten his horses from Egypt and was the first to introduce
the horse and chariot as a regular part of Israel's army.

What were Solomon's horses like? I discovered a partial
answer to this question in an article from the *Jewish Journal*
titled *The Solomon Project: New Israeli Breed of Horses.* In 1984,
Israel's horse breeders launched a new program to recreate
the biblical horse strain established by King Solomon.
(Many scholars believe that the modern Arab horse is
descended from this strain.)

The characteristics that have been selected for a distinctive
Israeli horse are similar to those Solomon prized:

*Hardy horses with superior endurance,
Spirited, but responsive to discipline,
Equally comfortable in the show-ring or
on the rugged trails of the Negev Desert
(A combination of pedigreed elegance and
desert ruggedness).*

The effort to breed a fine Israeli Arab horse will take about twenty years. A horse from the distinctive King Solomon line could be valued at more than $1,000,000.

How do we match up to the standards of Solomon's horses? Are we hardy, with superior endurance? Or do we faint with the first wind of adversity? Do we manifest the fruit of perseverance in our lives? Are we strong in the Lord and in the power of His might? Or are we spiritually frail and sickly?

What about spirit? Are we "salty" believers, letting our lights shine, walking in the Holy Spirit, ready in season and out to share the Word and life of the Lord with others? What about discipline? How quick are we to respond to the nudges of the Holy Spirit:

"Give them some money."
"Don't say that."
"Go another way."
"This is the wrong time."
"Call them now."

How about the tongue? Have we made progress in responding to the discipline of the Lord, as He teaches us when to speak and when not to speak, what to say and what not to say?

I pray that now that I'm over twenty years old in *Yeshua*, I have begun to learn some of these lessons. It is hard to imagine being worth more than $1,000,000, but we certainly are that valuable to our God!

We need to be as flexible and adaptable as Solomon's horses, trusting in God in all situations, knowing who we are in Him, being content with much or with little.

Especially dear to the heart of God is *a company of horses*. This could be symbolic of what I like to call a "bridal company": a group of believers bound together in perfect unity with the same goal, the same love, the same vision. If one of Solomon's horses was beautiful, imagine a whole

66

group of them running together!

This is a picture of the Bride of Messiah, made up of Jews, non-Jews, and believers from all denominations who answer to the call, *"O my love…"*

God wants *you* to be a part of that company!

$\mathcal{D}ay$ 33

Thy cheeks are comely with rows of jewels, thy neck with chains of gold. Song of Songs 1:10

Oriental brides in Bible times (and Yemenite Jewish brides today) wore strings of jewels which hung down over their cheeks in layers. The bride, adorned in this way, was considered beautiful. Some of the bride's jewels had been received as gifts at the time of betrothal, since this was the custom in ancient times (see Isaiah 61:10). Remember Rebekah, Isaac's bride? At her betrothal she was given *"jewels of silver and jewels of gold..."* (Genesis 24:53).

The nation of Israel was also given bridal jewels when the God of Abraham, Isaac, and Jacob purchased her as His own and took her by the hand to lead her out of Egypt. We read the following in Exodus 12:35 concerning that time in Israel's history: *"Now the children of Israel had done according to the word of Moses, and they had asked from the Egyptians articles of silver, articles of gold, and clothing."*

Jewels and brides go together. Today, a diamond is often given as a token of love and commitment. (Diamonds are Israel's number one export.) My husband never had to purchase a diamond for me. My mother offered him the one that my grandmother was given on her engagement.

Many of the other family jewels I owned were stolen in 1975. I was young in the Lord and still very attached to "things," especially old things. My family dates back to the time of the Mayflower, and many antiques and old jewelry were passed down from generation to generation. I kept my "jewels" in a box in my bedroom. One night I had a dream that the Messiah Jesus returned. He called to me, and I said, "Wait a moment. I have to get my jewelry."

Yeshua said, "You won't need them here."

About a month later, while we were out ministering to Jewish people, our townhouse was robbed. You guessed it. They took most of the old jewelry! I learned my first lesson about idolatry, and asked God to forgive me and set me free from a spirit of materialism and the bondage to things of this world.

The Lord began to teach me about true jewels. I discovered that the Torah (the Pentateuch, or Five Books of Moses) is called a many-faceted jewel. I began to see that the most precious jewels are those found in the Word of God — the teachings of the Holy Scriptures, both Old and New. These jewels should adorn the Bride of Messiah.

Jewels in the New Covenant Scriptures also encompass the gifts and the fruit of the Holy Spirit. Messiah's Bride should be adorned with love, joy, peace, long-suffering, kindness, goodness, faithfulness, gentleness, and self-control, and operate in the gifts given to her when *Yeshua* went back to be with His Father (Ephesians 4:8).

There is one more aspect to "jewels" that is only revealed as we examine the Hebrew word for *jewels* used in this verse. *Kley* (pronounced 'clay'), which just so happens to come from the same root word as *bride*, also means *weapons, armor, or vessels*. It's the word used to describe the utensils used for holy purposes in the Tabernacle in the wilderness: *Kley HaKodesh* or holy articles.

All of this paints a slightly different picture of the Bride. Now we see her as a warrior Bride, adorned with her weapons of warfare — the Word and the Spirit — with her helmet of salvation firmly in place, beautiful in the eyes of the Captain of her salvation. She is a chosen, holy vessel, brave, bold, and beautiful.

The Lord has more hidden jewels for you. *Seek and you shall find*! Worship the One who is *more precious than diamonds: Yeshua* HaMashiach!

Day 34

We will make thee borders of gold with studs of silver.   Song of Songs 1:11

The King is the one who has given the Shulamite the jewels. They are a gift from Him. In verse 11, He speaks of Himself in the plural, perhaps referring to Himself and His helpers. Sometimes the *We* found in the *Tanach* is referred to as *"the plural of majesty."* This is often a way to circumvent the numerous occurrences of the triune nature of God which appear throughout the Old Covenant Scriptures. One of these occurrences, *"...Let Us make man in Our image..."* (Genesis 1:26), made a deep impression upon my Jewish husband and eventually led him to conclude that *Yeshua* was the One promised to His people.

Father, Son, and Holy Spirit are all involved in the preparation of the Bride. The Father's divine nature (represented by gold), the Son's redemption (represented by silver), and the Holy Spirit's gifts (represented by the word *jewels*, see verse 10), are all gifts of One God manifested in three persons! Through redemption, we have become partakers of the Father's divine nature. The indwelling *Ruach HaKodesh* is the One who leads us, guides us, and teaches us about our Bridegroom/King. He helps us adorn ourselves with heavenly jewels.

Yeshua is coming back for a beautiful Bride. If left to ourselves, we would fail miserably at becoming what He wants us to be. Queen Esther has provided a model for us. When it was her turn to go in to the king, she requested nothing but what Hegai, the king's eunuch, the custodian of the women, advised: *"And Esther obtained favor in the sight of all who saw her"* (Esther 2:15).

Hegai is a type of the Holy Spirit. By being sensitive to

this helper whom God has given us, we will be led step by step in a spiritual beautification program, especially designed for each of us as individuals. *Trust* His leading! Yield to His Spirit. Let the cry of your heart be that of the Psalmist, who said, *"Let the beauty of the Lord be upon us ..."* (Psalm 90:17).

Not *our* beauty, but *His*. That is what counts in this life and the next. Our standard should be as different from the world's as day and night. The world looks at the outside (external beauty). God sees the heart (internal beauty). The world's beauty is natural. God's beauty is spiritual. The world's beauty fades with age. God's beauty increases with age. In 1 Peter chapter 3, verses 3 and 4, we read about the Lord's standard of beauty for women: *"Do not let your beauty be that outward adorning of arranging the hair, wearing gold, or of putting on fine apparel; but let it be the hidden person of the heart, with the incorruptible ornament of a gentle and quiet spirit, which is very precious in the sight of God..."*

How do we become adorned with the Lord's jewels?

How does Messiah's beauty appear in us? By drawing closer and closer to the source of beauty: *Yeshua*, Himself. There is no substitute for spending time alone with Him. Communion results in closeness and trust. Humility, yielding, obeying, and pursuing love are all part of the process of being conformed to His image.

Don't be discouraged. God sees His beauty in you already! Cling to Him. His Spirit will do the work!

$\mathcal{D}ay$ 35

While the king sitteth at his table ...
Song of Songs 1:12

Picture our Bridegroom King *Yeshua*: He is not away at war, fighting on the battlefield. He is not in a rush to get somewhere. He is not worried, anxious, or fearful. He is relaxed and in control. He is sitting at His table.

This verse is so rich that we need to spend two days meditating on it. In this first half of verse 12, there are three key words: *king, sitteth,* and *table. Yeshua* explained what type of a King He was at a table before His death. It was right before the Feast of Passover. Supper had ended. Our King rose from the table, laid aside His garments, took a towel, girded Himself, and washed His disciples' feet. Afterwards, He sat down again and explained to them that His kingdom was to be a kingdom of servant-lovers. As King, He had set the example. In *Yeshua's* kingdom, His followers should wash one another's feet.

At this moment, *Yeshua* is seated at the right hand of *HaG'vurah, the Power,* i.e. God (see Luke 22:69). We also read about *Yeshua's* exalted position in Hebrews 10:11-13: *"And every priest [cohen] stands ministering daily and offering repeatedly the same sacrifices, which can never take away sins. But this Man, after He had offered one sacrifice for sins forever, sat down at the right hand of God, from that time waiting til His enemies are made His footstool."*

Yeshua's work is finished. The work of redemption was completed on the tree of sacrifice. Our forgiveness was purchased, our healing provided for, our debt of sin was paid in full. *Yeshua* died, rose again, ascended to Heaven, and sat down.

Where is *Yeshua* sitting? I like to call His table "the King's table." Consider for a moment King Solomon's table: *"Now Solomon's provision for one day was 30 kors of fine flour, 60 kors of meal, 10 fatted oxen, 20 oxen from the pastures, and 100 sheep, besides deer, gazelles, roebucks, and fatted fowl"* (1 Kings 4:22-23). *Yeshua's* table is far greater than Solomon's table ever was! It has the provision for every need we will ever have. Our King's table overflows with sumptuous spiritual fare.

Yeshua's Bride has unlimited access to His table. It is prepared for us, even *"in the presence of our enemies"* (Psalm 23:5). At Messiah's table, we find nourishment for the soul, peace that passes understanding, all kinds of luscious spiritual fruit, living water, strength for the day, wisdom, power, and understanding. There is provision for whatever our need may be. And there is precious fellowship with the One who said, *"Behold, I stand at the door and knock. If anyone hears My voice and opens the door, I will come in to him and dine with him, and he with Me"* (Revelation 3:20).

This is the King's table. It becomes especially real to us when we celebrate the Lord's *seder* (also known as the Lord's Supper or Communion). It is here that, in partaking of the bread and wine, symbolizing Messiah's body and blood, we can most easily appropriate all that *Yeshua* longs to give us: reconciliation, forgiveness, healing, His love, His peace, His power to love, and much more!

Thank God for the King's table! *Yeshua* invites us to come and dine with Him. Sit down. He is sitting. Relax. Put all your cares and concerns aside for the moment, quiet your soul and allow the King to bless you at His table.

Day 36

...my spikenard sendeth forth the smell thereof.
Song of Songs 1:12

What does the Bride do at the King's table? First, she receives; then, she gives. What could we possibly give to a King who has everything? Our love, our lives, our very self. But before we can love God we must come to the realization of His love for us. The Scriptures make it clear that *"We love Him because He first loved us"* (1 John 4:19). A deep revelation of God's love for you will cause the following to spring up in your soul: joy, thankfulness, awe and wonder, and a desire to reciprocate love. The more you have been forgiven by *Yeshua*, the more you will love Him. The Shulamite is amazed that such a great King could ever love her. We should be amazed as well, but not so amazed that we shrink back from the One who, knowing all our faults, loves us most!

Upon realizing the depths of Jesus' love for me (I called him Jesus in 1976), I wrote a song entitled *"O How I Love the Way You Love Me."* The words to the chorus are as follows:

O, how I love the way You love me.
O, how I love the way You care.
O, how I love the way You come to me each day.
O, how I love the way You love!

I was at the King's table when I wrote that song. I also happened to be seated at my piano. I was alone with God. No one else was in the house. I had been still before Him for awhile, meditating on His Word, thinking about His love for me, and realizing that I didn't deserve it. I related to all the Marys in the Bible at that season of my life and

74

delighted in sitting at the Lord's feet listening to His words. I wanted to do what Mary the sister of Lazarus did while the King sat at His table. We read in John 12:3 that she took a pound of very costly oil of spikenard (an aromatic plant used as a perfume) and anointed the feet of *Yeshua*, and wiped His feet with her hair. The house was filled with the fragrance of the oil. My way of expressing love was to write a song to my King.

Mary's act of love was certainly more lavish than mine. One pound of spikenard cost 300 *dinarii*, nearly a year's wages. This act of sacrificial love on Mary's part evoked great anger from Judas Iscariot (see John 12:4-6). Bridal love will, many times, inflame the Judas spirit. If you love *Yeshua* extravagantly, you will probably be criticized. Keep loving anyway! Bow before your King. Let your heart attitude be one of humble adoration. Be willing to break the alabaster box that contains the precious ointment as another Mary did, as recorded in Mark 14:3. This Mary broke the flask and poured the costly oil on the Messiah's head.

The alabaster box of our self-life must be broken before a sweet fragrance can come forth. We must come to the place where we see our own nothingness and unworthiness. We must come to the realization that without Him we are nothing. But with Him, we are a special new creation! This is the grace of God!

Let us pray together today:

> *O God! Pour out your grace upon me that I might yield my life completely to You. I desire to say "no" to pride, self-pity, arrogance, selfishness, and every other evil that would prevent me from worshipping you in humility and love.*   *In Yeshua's Name,*
> *Amen.*

Day 37

A bundle of myrrh is my well-beloved unto me...
Song of Songs 1:13

Myrrh is an oily resin that oozes naturally from the stems of Commiphora, a thorny shrub or small tree that did not grow in the land of Israel in Bible times. Myrrh was therefore imported from India, Arabia, or Africa, making it very costly and precious.

Bitter in taste but very fragrant, myrrh was used in medicine and was an important ingredient in holy oils and cosmetics. Myrrh is sold as a spice in the Middle East today, and is still used there as a medicine.

In Bible times, myrrh was a very valuable and desirable substance. There are a number of allusions to this throughout the Holy Scriptures. In The Song of Songs alone, myrrh is mentioned in seven verses. In the New Covenant Scriptures, myrrh is related to both the birth and death of the Messiah.

Even before He was born, myrrh was linked prophetically to *Yeshua*. The Psalmist expressed it as follows in Psalm 45, a Messianic Wedding Song: *"All Your garments are scented with myrrh, and aloes, and cassia..."* (Psalm 45:8). At His birth, wise men brought the infant Jesus myrrh as well as gold and frankincense (Matthew 2:11). At His death, Nicodemus brought a mixture of myrrh and aloes to the tomb of *Yeshua* (John 19:39). In life as well as in death, *Yeshua*'s garments were fragranced with myrrh.

What is the spiritual significance of myrrh? During Temple times, Hebrew people in Israel used myrrh as a common pain killer. As such, it is symbolic of *Yeshua*'s ministry of healing. Our well-beloved *Yeshua*, the Messiah, heals bodies, wounded spirits, and broken hearts. *He* is a bundle of myrrh to each member of His Bride.

One of the most precious passages in the Bible to me is Mark 15:22,23,25: *"And they brought Him to the place Golgotha, which is translated, Place of a Skull. Then they gave Him wine mingled with myrrh to drink, but He did not take it ...Now it was the third hour, and they crucified Him."*

Yeshua was offered myrrh right before they crucified Him—to help deaden the pain, but He refused it. Love refused it. He chose to bear *all* the pain for us. He took *all* our sins upon Himself. As the Prophet Isaiah says so beautifully in Isaiah 53:5: *"But He was wounded for our transgressions, He was bruised for our iniquities; the chastisement for our peace was upon Him, and by His stripes we are healed."*

In a wonderful little book, *Jesus Bore Our Sorrows* by David Alsobrook, the author summarizes what *Yeshua* did for us: "He refused that natural myrrh in this life so that you can partake of spiritual myrrh."

What about the bundle? It was customary to gather the stems of the plant and tie them into bundles of sticks. The natural sap would ooze out and be used as ointment. Think of each stick in that bundle as an aspect of *Yeshua's* healing ministry. He is the healer of disappointments, broken relationships, grief, rejection, abuse, as well as the healer of cancer, depression, stress, and all manner of sorrows and afflictions.

Our well-beloved is a healing Savior. *For the joy set before Him,* He took the bitterness upon Himself. No bitterness should be found in His Bride. We must embrace the myrrh and appropriate His sweetness and His fragrance. Be refreshed, comforted, soothed, and healed in the Name of *Yeshua* today. *By His stripes we are healed!*

Day 38

...he shall lie all night betwixt my breasts.
Song of Songs 1:13

Night in The Song of Songs symbolizes *separation, trial, testing, or pain*. Night is a difficult time for many people today — a lonely time, a fear-filled time. When our son Jesse was five years old, he began to experience fear in the night. Going to bed was no problem, but going to sleep was. Jesse didn't like being alone. He was sure there were "ghosties" under the bed. Darkness terrified him. He insisted on having two night lights. When we told him that *Yeshua* was right there in bed with him, he protested, saying, "He may be, but He doesn't have skin!" Prayer, some spiritual warfare, and soothing spiritual tapes helped. Jesse was comforted by God's Holy Spirit as the Light of the World dispelled the darkness.

Is the Messiah with us in the dark times of our lives? Yes. He is closer then than perhaps at any other time. *All* night long, He is close to our heart. He knows that we need Him. Even when we are not aware, He is still close to us, for He has said: *"I will never leave you nor forsake you"* (Hebrews 13:5). We may not feel the skin, but *Yeshua* can make Himself very real to us through the *Ruach HaKodesh*.

Jewish sources tell us that in antiquity, a flask containing perfume (*klee shel bosem*) was worn by women around the neck. It hung down below the breast. Myrrh may have been used in such a flask, even in the night.

Yeshua manifested Himself during a nighttime season in the life of a friend of ours, a Messianic Rabbi's wife, who experienced a physical trial which many experience today: cancer. From an unexplained pain in the shoulder to a misdiagnosis of sarcoma to a final diagnosis of plasmacytoma (bone marrow cancer), Angela held onto God (actually, God held onto Angela). She felt that there was something she had to learn from what was going on in her body. One morning at 5:00 A.M., she arose and asked the Lord what He wanted her to do. Angela didn't understand why everything was happening, but she knew that God was with her. The Lord gave her a battle plan in the wee hours of the morning. He told her that there is no victory without a battle. The battlefield was her body. Prayer was going to be the most important weapon and of utmost importance. The battle was the Lord's!

Angela understood the Lord saying to her that her flesh would grow weary, but that she should hold fast, be diligent, and persevere. Other instructions included not giving in to a spirit of fear, submitting to God and to her doctors, taking responsibility for her own health, meditating on the Word of God, and committing everything to *Yeshua*.

Angela related to me how the Lord's presence overwhelmed her on the table as they did the biopsy on her shoulder. Confidence and total peace enveloped her as the procedure came to an end. Angela decided to praise the Lord no matter what was going on in her body. She decided, "I am healed if I can praise Him!"

At the end of two months, the plasmacytoma on the shoulder was no longer a problem. Angela had gone through radiation with no side effects. Her final comment to me about the Lord during this nighttime experience was this: "God is *so* real!"

Yes, He is.

P.S. Angela's battle is not over, but *Yeshua* is closer than ever. When darkness threatens, His light gets brighter.

Day 39

My beloved is unto me as a cluster of camphire in the vineyards of Engedi. Song of Songs 1:14

Just as *Yeshua* is myrrh in the night, He is living water in the desert. Engedi is a magnificent oasis in the midst of the Judean Desert. The first time I saw Engedi, I was shocked. We had been driving for at least a half hour through barren, sandy, rocky, mountainous lands. The heat was intense—hotter even than South Florida! I wasn't prepared to look out the bus window and see a lush garden right ahead of us with mile after mile of date palm trees, orange trees, pomelos, and other fruit trees. We were at the shore of the Dead Sea. How could there be so much life here? Doesn't the Bible call Engedi a *"wilderness"* (1 Samuel 24:1)? (I realized that *wilderness* meant it was far removed from the great population centers of Israel.) Engedi is more like a garden than a wilderness.

The word *camphire* in this verse is more correctly translated from the Hebrew as *henna*. Henna grew in abundance in Engedi and gave off a strong, sweet scent. According to the rabbis, *cluster of henna* refers allegorically to atonement and pardon since the word *henna* in Hebrew means *ransom price*. It comes from the root *kaphar, to cover*. In a Messianic context, a cluster of henna would refer to *Yeshua*, our ransom price.

Yeshua is our atonement. Through Him we are at one with God. *Yeshua* is also living water in the midst of a spiritual desert. The majestic waterfalls of Engedi remind us of that living water and of the promise given to us by our Messiah in John 7:37-38: *"If anyone thirsts, let him come to Me and drink. He who believes in Me, as the Scripture has said, out of his heart will flow rivers of living water."*

The *cluster of henna* — all that's included in the atonement — is God's will for each of us today. Forgiveness of sins, peace with God, assurance of eternal life, the indwelling of God's *Ruach HaKodesh*, adoption into God's family, access to God twenty-four hours a day, precious promises from the Word of God, abundant life here on earth, and healing for body, soul, and spirit are all included in the *atonement cluster*.

God is not a stingy God. He is the Giver of *every good and perfect gift*. He is a lavish Giver. Why not try something fun and foolish today? Take a shower. Let the water be the waterfalls of Engedi and the gifts of God included in *Yeshua*'s atonement. Praise the Lord for His desire to pour out His goodness upon you. Praise the Lord for the atonement and all that it means in your life. Praise the Lord for His living water and the outpouring of His Holy Spirit in your life. Praise the Lord for the washing of water by the Word (Ephesians 5:26). Praise the Lord for cleansing you from all iniquity through the blood of *Yeshua*. Praise the Lord for *Yeshua* — your atonement, the One who paid the price for your salvation.

Allow love for *Yeshua* to penetrate your being. Realize His preciousness. Confess that He alone can satisfy. Continue to hunger and thirst after righteousness. You will be filled. God has promised to pour water on the one who is thirsty!

Day 40

Behold, thou art fair, my love; behold, thou art fair...   Song of Songs 1:15

The Messiah now expresses His love for His Bride. She has praised her Beloved, and now He praises her. He calls her His *love, rayati* in Hebrew, and repeats twice that she is *fair*. The Hebrew word for *fair* that is used in this verse is *yaphah* (pronounced 'ya-FAH'), a primary root which means *to be bright or beautiful*. God certainly understands women. He created them. He knows that women need to hear that they are beautiful in the eyes of the one who loves them. As we teach marriage seminars, Neil and I usually mention that men are aroused and stimulated by what they see, and women by what they hear. We tell the story of the woman who says to her husband: "Honey, do you love me?" He responds: "Of course, I love you. I told you that twenty years ago when I married you!" That's not enough for most women. They want more *words*!

Yeshua is generous with His words. He tells His Bride that she is beautiful, not once, but twice. The rabbinic interpretations apply this declaration of beauty to God's love relationship with Israel. One commentator says that the repetition of the phrase "you are beautiful" refers to the past and present. Israel became beautiful when she received the Torah on Mount Sinai, and she is still beautiful.

In a Messianic sense, we could say that each of us, as believers, became beautiful when we received the Messiah as our own. And in God's eyes, we are still beautiful!

It's hard to imagine that the same word *fair*, used to describe the Messiah in Psalm 45 would also be used to describe each of us. But it is. In Messiah's case, however, He is not only *fair*, He is *fairer* than the sons of men (Psalm 45:2).

Whatever is beautiful in us is a reflection of *His* beauty. *Yeshua* sees us through eyes of love. We are His beloved Bride. He purchased us with His own blood. We are of great value to Him.

Have you ever seen an ugly bride? I haven't. There is no such thing as an ugly bride! A bride is always beautiful because love surrounds her. She loves, and she is loved. The knowledge of this has real transforming power.

A story is told of a farmer on an island in the Pacific who had two daughters. The younger daughter was very beautiful, and the older daughter was not. No one wanted to marry the older daughter. The usual procedure was that a bride had to be purchased. The going price was a cow, but this girl was so plain that the farmer despaired of ever having his daughter marry and ever having the cow. One day the wealthiest bachelor on the island, who was also very handsome, visited the farmer and said: "I would like to marry your oldest daughter."

The farmer said: "You're prepared to pay 1 cow for her?"

The handsome bachelor said: "Absolutely not! She is worth much more. I insist on paying 10 cows for her!"

The farmer could not believe his ears, but he accepted the offer. The marriage was consummated. The bride left with her husband. About a year later, the farmer was startled to see his son-in-law returning with a beautiful woman by his side. The farmer asked, "What have you done with my daughter?"

"This is your daughter," the groom replied!

A great love can make *anyone* beautiful!

We are *fair* (beautiful) in the eyes of *Yeshua* because He loves us, because He purchased us, because we are new creations in Him, clothed with the righteousness that comes through faith, and because He sees us as we shall be one day—like Himself—*the perfection of beauty.*

Agree with God and His opinion of you. Share God's opinion of His Bride with a brother or sister in the Lord. Minister life, grace, and beauty. Let everything that happens today be colored by this glorious truth: You are beautiful to God!

Day 41

...thou hast doves' eyes.   Song of Songs 1:15

The Hebrew word for *dove* is *yonah*. It comes from the same root as the word *yayin* which means *wine*. Although at first glance, there is no apparent connection between doves and wine, we find in the Holy Scriptures a definite correlation. Both *the dove* and *wine* are used as a symbol of the Holy Spirit. The *wine* is the "new wine" of God's *Ruach* as found in the New Covenant Scriptures.

The dove as a symbol of the Holy Spirit is found both in the *Tanach* and in the *Brit HaDasha*. The Spirit of God is the Spirit of peace. The first mention of this Spirit is found in the biblical account of creation where the Spirit of God *hovered* above the surface of the waters — like a *dove*.

That same Spirit continues to hover over each "new" creation that is supernaturally born into the Kingdom of God. It also hovers over each "bridal-soul," preparing God's people to meet the Heavenly Bridegroom, *Yeshua*. Every member of the Bride also has this dove-like Spirit on the inside, through regeneration and spiritual rebirth in Messiah.

How does God detect the presence of His Spirit in His Bride? Through her eyes! There is an ancient rabbinic teaching which says that the eyes are an index of character. A bride who has beautiful eyes possesses a beautiful personality. The Bride of Messiah is beautiful as she reflects the beauty of the Lover of her soul. His beauty has been imparted to her through the Holy Spirit. As Messiah's Bride yields more and more to the Spirit of God, more and more of His beauty is seen in her. This happens when the eyes of the Bride become like the eyes of the *dove*.

What exactly are *doves' eyes* like? First of all, they are the most prominent feature of the bird. They are large and round.

I'll never forget the birthday I asked the Lord for a *dove* so that I could see its eyes up close. My parents were visiting from New York. My dad didn't believe in all my "spiritual activities." I told him that I was waiting for a *dove* to arrive. He made some comments about that—until a beautiful *dove* flew into our backyard and sat in a black olive tree for most of the afternoon. Each time I approached it, it just sat still staring at me. I kept saying to my father: "Look at those eyes, Daddy!" He kept shaking his head (my dad, not the *dove*).

Doves have no peripheral vision. They can only see straight ahead. They can only focus on one thing at a time. We need to be this focused. The Scriptures tell us, in Hebrews 12:1-2, that Messiah's Bride must put aside every impediment, every distraction, every sideways glance, and press forward, running with endurance, looking always to the Author and Finisher of our faith, *Yeshua*, the Messiah. In other words, *we must keep our eyes on Him! He* is the lighthouse that will show us the way in the storm. He is the prize at the end of the race. He is the goal, the high mark, the target. Only Jesus.

Doves mate for life. They are noted for their faithfulness and gentleness. This is where the term "lovey dovey" comes from. Messiah's Bride must have the gentle, faithful nature of the *dove*. As we await the return of the Bridegroom, we must be found faithful, having eyes only for the Beloved. The temptation to have wandering eyes is great. The world offers tantalizing trinkets. The marketplace assaults us with temptation on every side. Don't compromise! Be true to *Yeshua*! Be careful what you let your eyes take in! Resist the devil. Look the other way when materialism, greed, lust, pride, and selfish gain seek to entice you!

Ask the Lord to give you *doves' eyes*! This will touch His heart. He longs to see faithfulness in His people. This fruit of the Spirit, this *dove*-like quality, is an important part of the adorning of the end-time Bride. The Lord has betrothed His people to Himself *in faithfulness* (Hosea 2:20). Wouldn't it be wonderful if *we* could live our lives in such a way that one day He would say to us: *"Great is thy faithfulness!"*

Let's endeavor to delight our King!

$\mathcal{D}ay$ 42

Behold, thou art fair, my beloved, yea, pleasant:
also our bed is green.   Song of Songs 1:16

The compliment that the Bridegroom gives the Bride in verse 15 is returned in verse 16. Now she calls Him *fair* (beautiful) and addresses Him as her *Beloved*. He is *pleasant* (delightful, sweet) to her. Here we see the reciprocal praises of The Song of Songs. There is a mutual building up, a healthy relationship where communication is open and positive.

Believers know that the Bible teaches us to praise the Lord. How do we do this? What do we say? The Song of Songs provides us with wonderful words of love to use in communicating our deepest feelings to the Lover of our soul. Have you ever told the Lord how beautiful, sweet, and delightful He is? Try using some of the words from this Song today as you spend time with the Lord in prayer. Just saying *"Yeshua, my Beloved..."* and then waiting in His presence can usher you into a sweet time of sitting at His feet! Remember: *"...He [God] made us accepted in the Beloved"* (Ephesians 1:6). We are the object of His desire. We were chosen in Him before the foundation of the world (Ephesians 1:4). The Beloved never rejects His Bride. He is more wonderful than words can express!

The Bride goes on to say that she and the Beloved have a *green* bed. What could this possibly mean? The word *green* in Hebrew which is used here, *raanan*, means *green, fresh or flourishing*. A pastoral setting is brought to mind. The Bride and her Beloved have a budding relationship. Their communion is flourishing. Perhaps they find themselves in a beautiful country setting where lush green foliage and trees of the field abound.

My own personal relationship with *Yeshua* has been greatly enhanced by those times I have spent with Him in an outdoor nature setting. Sometimes it has been by the sea, other times in a garden, or even in a tree! In October of 1993, I spoke at a Messianic women's retreat in San Diego, California. The location of the retreat was a beautiful woodsy setting surrounded by mountains. Outside the dining room, there was a huge oak tree, just perfect for climbing. I resisted for most of the retreat (after all, it might be strange if any of the ladies found the guest speaker up in a tree) but finally came to the proper conclusion: "Why not? Perhaps I'll see *Yeshua* as Zacchaeus did."

It was a wonderful tree to sit in, and I was delighted to find a plaque on the trunk of the tree that said: *"Prayer Tree."* I spent quite a while talking to the Lord in that tree. It was so beautiful. *He* was so beautiful. I asked Him about my life. I questioned Him about my calling and poured out my heart to Him. I felt overwhelmed with the various demands on my time: marriage, children, home, TV program, newsletters, speaking engagements, travel, etc., etc.. I said to the Lord, "What am I *really* called to do?" He told me to look at the tree—that my calling was the same as its calling—TO POINT PEOPLE TO GOD. Not very complicated, I thought. I dried my tears and really felt much better when I climbed down.

I had had an intimate encounter with my Lord. Truly our bed had been *green*. As a reminder of that time, I'm in the process of putting some green plants in my bedroom. When Neil asks me what I'm doing, I'll tell him it has to do with Song of Songs 1:16. He'll remind me that the marriage bed should always be *green*. Yes, we wives must remember to cultivate both levels of intimacy — the intimacy of *Yeshua* and His bride, as well as the intimacy between husbands and wives.

Lord, thank You for times apart with You in the beautiful world that You've created. Please provide special opportunities for me to have intimate fellowship with You, so that I can say: 'Our bed is green.'

Wives, take this opportunity to pray about your own "marriage bed." Ask the Father to keep it *green*. Read The Song of Songs with your husband. On a purely literal level, it has much to offer married couples. The first time I realized this, I blushed. Then I began suggesting that couples share The Song on their honeymoon. We end our marriage retreats with this closing thought: *The best thing you can do to improve your marriage relationship is to improve your relationship with God.*

The Song of Songs can help with both relationships.

$\mathcal{D}ay$ 43

The beams of our house are cedar, and our rafters
of fir.   Song of Songs 1:17

The word *our* in *our house* is used in verse 17 as it was in the previous verse in *our bed,* referring to the progressive realization of oneness that the Bride and the Bridegroom are experiencing. They are building a relationship. They are building a life together. It is a divine construction. The Maker and Builder is the Lord God of Israel Himself.

Traditional Jewish commentators say that the *house* in this verse refers to the Tabernacle or the Temple in Jerusalem, the dwelling place of God. The great Jewish expositor Rashi explains that the existence of the Temple in Israel led to flourishing, vigorous (*green*) growth of the Jewish population. The Temple symbolizes the intimacy that existed between God and Israel.

Solomon used cedar wood in building the Temple because of its superior quality, fragrance, and durability. The rabbis say that the Temple which shall be built in the days of King Messiah, shall be even more beautiful, with beams of the cedars of the Garden of Eden, and pillars of firs, juniper, and cypress wood.

There is no Jewish Temple today. It was destroyed by the Romans in 70 A.D. So, where does God dwell now? Where is His tabernacle? Where is His home? The answer is simple yet profound. His home is the human heart. God now dwells in temples of His Spirit, temples not made by human hands. Through *Yeshua,* divinity dwells within humanity.

The Messiah, speaking about the *Ruach HaKodesh* shortly before His death, said to His disciples, *"...but you know Him, for He dwells with you, and will be in you"* (John 14:17).

The home we are building with our Lord has as its

foundation Yeshua the Messiah Himself. It is not a relationship established on shifting sand. The winds may blow. The storm may rage. Hurricanes and tornados may increase in frequency and intensity, but our home in *Yeshua* will stand firm.

Cedar is not only a "royal" wood; it is also a wood that is highly "resistant" to pests and decay. The home we are building in the Spirit is also highly resistant. Our God has caused us to triumph in Messiah over all the works of the enemy.

Fir trees (actually, Evergreen Cypress) were tall, stately, beautiful trees. Solomon used them along with cedar when he built the Temple. Like the stately fir, *having done all, [we] stand* (Ephesians 6:13).

Perhaps you've never thought of yourself as building a home (life) together with the Lord. This truth is especially important for young people and those who are single or widowed to comprehend. You are involved in an exciting adventure with God! *Together* you are creating something majestic, beautiful, and eternal. Like the magnificent cedars, it is deeply rooted, strong, and designed to last a long, long time. You are not alone.

Devote yourself to the service of the One who builds with you. Spend many hours in His presence. Discuss plans, share dreams, choose materials, dispense funds with Him. One day you may build a home of your own in the natural. There's no better preparation for that than building your spiritual home today with *Yeshua*.

Enjoy the process!

and

Grow *like a cedar* (Psalm 92:12).

$\mathcal{D}ay$ 44

I am the rose of Sharon...   Song of Songs 2:1

Today we begin meditating on Song of Songs chapter 2 where we have our first introduction to the rose of Sharon. Before contemplating the rose, I would like to establish its place in the overall context of this special chapter.

Over the years, I have monitored my own spiritual progress, chapter by chapter in The Song of Songs. For many years (perhaps five or six), I felt as if I was living in chapter 2. I would read it over and over and say, "That's me!" I have become acutely aware of a journey that my soul embarked upon the day I met the Messiah. The Song is the story of my journey. I long to reach chapter 8, for it is here that *Yeshua* returns for His Bride!

The Bride does a lot of talking in chapter 2. She is occupied with herself and is like many believers today who are concerned about their own needs being met. They desire to receive ministry rather than minister to others, to be fed rather than feed others. This is a normal part of growing up in Messiah. It only becomes a problem if development is arrested at this stage.

Yeshua loves the infant "bridal-soul" who wants everything he or she can get from God and realizes how totally dependent he is on God to supply. The joyful exuberance of "I don't deserve any of this! Who am I that God would do all this for me? But I love it!" is a sweet sound to the ear of our Heavenly Father.

This is the humility of *the rose*. The Bride says she is *the rose of Sharon*. An entire treatise could be written on the word *rose* in this verse! It has been variously translated as *crocus, tulip, iris, narcissus, anemone, and rose*. Since many Orthodox Jewish commentators, as well as the authors of the book, *The History of the Rose in the Holy Land Throughout the Ages,* believe that *the rose* is an actual rose in some form, I'm comfortable with that conclusion.

The Shulamite maiden is making a statement of humility when she calls herself a *rose.* She sees herself as the common wild rose of the Sharon plain (the coastal area from Caesarea to Joppa). In her own eyes she is nothing special, certainly not worthy of the affections of a great king. Who is she that the King of all Israel would set His love upon her? In the same way, we can ask who little Israel is that God decided to choose her, woo her, marry her, provide for her, forgive her, preserve her, and still have a plan for her? And who are *we,* that the King of all Kings has chosen each one of us to be His treasured possession?

Grace, pure grace. God chooses whom He will. He has chosen *you.* You are His *rose!* In traditional Christian circles, Jesus is called *The Rose of Sharon* based on this verse. The Hebrew, however, is definitely in the feminine. Since we are *one* with the Beloved, we *both* are *the rose.* It is His beauty, His fragrance, and His life in us. Messiah has made us what He is.

I surround myself with roses: real roses, artificial roses, dried roses, rose petals. We use a rose in the logo for our ministry, *"Jewish Jewels."* Those who intercede for our ministry are called Prayer Roses. The rose is a powerful symbol of LOVE and especially of God's love. Many years ago, I read a poem titled *It Was You, God, Who Ordered Roses For the World!* by Dr. Leo M. Jones:

> *To survive*
> *I must want to survive*
> *It is beauty that leads me*
> *To desire to continue infinitely.*
> *The beauty of a rose*
> *Is exciting in and of itself,*
> *But when the rose*
> *Has been given*
> *As an expression of love,*

Its beauty is irresistible.
It incorporates
The beauty of a human being
As well as its own beauty.
It was You, God,
Who ordered roses for the world!
They are an expression
Of your love.
Realizing this,
The beauty of a rose
Never fails to lift my heart,
Set it racing,
Awaken my desire
For infinite beauty.
The beauty of God Himself
Flashes forth in each rose.
Yet how many years
Did I look on roses before
Discovering this beauty?

This poem continues to make me smile. If no one else orders roses for you, God already has!

Trust God to send *you* roses. (It just so happens that as I write today, a gorgeous pink rose bush blooms outside my office door. It was given to us last week by our next door neighbors.)

"Thank you, Father, for roses!

Thank you, that in the Beloved, *I* am a beautiful rose!"

$\mathcal{D}ay$ 45

... and the lily of the valleys.   Song of Songs 2:1

The Bride now calls herself a *lily, shoshana* in Hebrew. *Shoshana* is an interesting word. It can also mean *rose,* and in fact is translated as such in the *Art Scroll Tanach Series* version of The Song. Roses and lilies are often interchangeable in Hebrew thought.

Most authorities believe that *the lily* spoken of in Song of Songs 2:1 is actually the Anemone Coronaria, or the Poppy Anemone. This little flower is a member of the buttercup family. Its flowers may be scarlet, crimson, purple, blue, or white. We have seen anemones carpet the Israeli countryside in the springtime, even bursting forth from every conceivable crack in the rocks. They may be "common," but they are very striking.

Bible scholars generally agree that the Messiah was referring to the anemone when He said: *"So why do you worry about clothing? Consider the lilies of the field, how they grow: they neither toil nor spin; and yet I say unto you that even Solomon in all his glory was not arrayed like one of these"* (Matthew 6:28-29).

If we consider this verse in the context of our Song we can picture King Solomon in his splendid royal apparel contrasted with the Shulamite maiden, humble and lowly, yet adorned with a glory that surpassed his. She was clothed like this through no effort of her own. She didn't *toil* or *spin* to get that way. What a lesson for us to learn! God wants us to stop our toiling and our spinning and allow *Him* to do a work in us. It is the Spirit of the Living God indwelling each member of His Bride that makes her *"all glorious within"* (Psalm 45:13).

Although the anemone is most probably *the lily* referred to in this verse, some scholars and writers (like me) feel that it is also appropriate to draw a comparison between the Bride and the *lily* as most of us know it today, the Lilium Candidum or White Madonna Lily. This *lily* is white and fragrant. Its pure whiteness brings to mind the purity of the soul redeemed by Messiah's blood. It speaks of the pure in heart, those who see God.

The *lily* holds water in its cup, and so do "bridal-souls." The source of water is pure and clear as crystal. It is the Messiah Himself, the Fountain of Living Waters, the same water that flowed from a Rock in the wilderness that gave drink to God's people Israel.

"Bridal-souls" are "*lily*-souls." I picture the "Bride of Christ" as being composed of millions of "*lily*-souls" of every color, race, tongue, size, shape, and age! We are a holy people unto the Lord. We are righteous. We are cleansed. We are fragrant — like the *lily*. We bloom where the Father has planted us — often in *the valley* instead of on the mountaintop. There are more of us than can be numbered. Our very existence should proclaim: "There is a Creator who has made me, who loves the world He made and longs to communicate with His creation."

This is what "*lily*-souls" do. They cause others to look to the Creator. This is a holy calling.

"Blessed [are] the pure in heart, for they shall see God" (Matthew 5:8).

Day 46

As the lily among thorns...　　　Song of Songs 2:2

When the Bride tells her Beloved that she is "just" a simple common flower, she is expressing a lingering doubt concerning His love for her. *He* loves *me*? Many believers in *Yeshua* experience this same nagging feeling. Some never allow it to rise to the surface so that God can remove it once and for all. If you are numbered in this group, allow the Lord to do a work in your heart today!

Your childhood may have been far less then ideal. You may never have known the unconditional love of a father or a mother. You may have experienced constant criticism, neglect, or abuse at a tender age. God is greater than all of these. In His Son, *Yeshua*, you are a new creation. The Beloved, speaking in this verse, sees you through eyes of love as a *lily among thorns*. The Messiah sees His own life already being manifested in you. To the Shulamite, the *lily* is of no great value. To the One who loves her, it is a flower of exquisite beauty.

We've contemplated the *lily* already, but what about the *thorns*? The first mention of *thorns* in the Holy Scriptures is found in Genesis 3:18 where we read of the temptation and the fall of man. God told Adam that because of his disobedience to the voice of God, the ground would be cursed. He would have to toil over it all the days of his life, and it would bring forth *thorns* and thistles. *Thorns* are a result of being cursed. *Thorns* are ugly, painful, and unpleasant. We read in Proverbs 22:5: *"Thorns and snares are in the way of the perverse; He who guards his soul will be far from them."*

Yeshua's Bride is blessed and is called to be a blessing. She is a *lily* in the midst of a perverse generation. She is light in the midst of darkness, life in the face of death, beauty in a world filled with ugliness, the fragrance of forgiveness instead of the stench of sin. All this and more is a *lily among thorns*!

Our calling in Scripture is sure. We read the following, in Philippians 2:14-16, in which the Apostle Paul (Rabbi Saul) urges believers to work *out* their own salvation with fear and trembling as God works *in* them *to will and do His good pleasure*: *"Do all things without murmuring and disputing, that you may become blameless and harmless, children of God without fault in the midst of a crooked and perverse generation, among whom you shine as lights in the world, holding fast the word of life..."*

I thought I had gotten rid of all my thorny tendencies (the old nature) until the Lord moved us into a large house on Fort Lauderdale beach and sent "His children" to live with us. For eleven years, He used other believers (mainly Jewish women, ages twenty to thirty) to show me how many *thorns* still needed to be removed! That obviously wasn't enough! He then proceeded to send us two children to refine us even further. We still have some *thorns,* but the Lord, in His abundant mercy, smells the *lily*! He is *so* good!

Your destiny is to be a *lily among thorns*. The world must see (and smell) the *lily*! Yield to the Spirit of God as He shows you areas in your life that are "thorny." They must be crucified — put to death — and resurrection life will follow. You will be perceived as a *"lily*-soul." You will refresh rather than wound others. Is this what you desire?

Surrender!

Day 47

The Beloved calls His Bride His *"Love."* This word for *love*, *rayati* in Hebrew, implies *a close friend-type of relationship.* It reminds me of the verse in the New Covenant in John 15:15 in which *Yeshua* tells His disciples about a new level of intimacy He will share with them: *"No longer do I call you servants, for a servant does not know what his master is doing; but I have called you friends, for all things that I heard from My Father I have made known to you."*

Are you His friend? Does the Lord share His plans, His hopes, His dreams, and His heart with you? Yesterday morning, as I sat at the piano worshipping the Lord, He spoke to me about His grief over the spirit of adultery that is sweeping through our country and even through the Body of Messiah. Multitudes of people are missing the mark, falling short of the good things that God wants to give them. They are living far below His standards, forfeiting the love, joy, and peace He longs to give in abundance. They are believing a lie.

I wondered about God sharing this burden with me. Then I realized that He wanted me to phone a sister in the Lord who had been ensnared by the enemy and tell her that God wanted her—desired her—and longed for closeness with her once more.

This morning, a young man came to fix our roof. Before I knew what was happening, we got into a conversation about the end-times which led to the disclosure of an adulterous relationship that he is presently involved in. I felt led to confront him with his sin and share that God has a better idea for his life. The Holy Spirit ministered in a gentle, quiet way as a standard of righteousness was lifted up. I realized how important it is to find out what's on God's heart. We need to be a good friend to Him, just as He is to us!

How do we, as *Yeshua*'s friends, relate to *the daughters*? How does the church relate to Israel? Historically, the church has not been a very good friend to Israel. She has not given off a *lily*-like fragrance. Instead, persecution and anti-Semitism have been the experience of the Jew when relating to the church. Neil remembers his mother telling him about her brother who made the mistake of walking past a church in Poland on an Easter Sunday morning. A group of young men saw him and called out, "Let's kill the Jew. He killed our Christ." They beat him to death in front of the church.

The *real* believers in Jesus as Messiah would never be involved in such an atrocity. The *real* Bride of the Lamb knows about and loves her Jewish roots and embraces a calling to love and comfort the Jewish people. The *real* friend of *Yeshua* also, with sensitivity, shares the glorious Gospel of Messiah with the House of Israel. How else can we give them *beauty for ashes, the oil of joy instead of mourning, or the garment of praise for the spirit of heaviness*? *Yeshua* is *their* Messiah, the only One who can remove the thorns that have pierced their heart over the ages.

Many times Christians shy away from Jewish people. They don't understand them. They seem "different." This is true, to a certain extent. Native-born Israelis are called *sabras*. The *sabra* is *a type of cactus with huge spines or thorns protruding from it*. Israelis are called *sabras* because they tend to have a rough, abrupt, tell-it-like-it-is exterior. Just like the fruit of the *sabra*, however, they are soft and sweet on the inside. God's people were designed by Him to be "survivors." Living among them since 1973 has caused me to appreciate their special resilience. I always "go for the heart" with Jewish people. If there are thorns in the way, I ask the Lord to show me the way around them.

God has not forgotten *the daughters* of Jerusalem. They were His first love. They committed spiritual adultery, and so have we; but God forgives. We both can be restored and become His *friends*.

Day 48

As the apple tree among the trees of the wood, so is my beloved among the sons...
Song of Songs 2:3

This is the first of four references to *the apple* in The Song of Songs. *The apple* of the Bible, like *the rose* and *the lily*, is a puzzling problem of correct botanical identification. Over the centuries, heated debate has revolved around *the apple* and *the apple tree*. Since this verse is one of my very favorites, I refuse to get involved in the debate, and I have chosen to agree with many of the scholars through the ages who contend that the common apple, Malus pumila, is the apple of the Scriptures.

But whether *the apple tree* referred to here is really an apple, or an apricot, a pomegranate, a citron, or an orange, the point that the Shulamite maiden is making about her Beloved is still the same: "He is the *best*! He is the greatest! There's no one quite like Him!" I agree! Can you picture the Messiah, *Yeshua*, as an *apple tree*?

The Bible is filled with metaphors about people and trees. Many years ago, I began to study some of those trees in the Bible. I contemplated the tree in the Garden of Eden that brought death, thanked God for the tree of death (Calvary) that brought life, and culminated my study with the tree in the Book of Revelation whose leaves are *for the healing of the nations*. I found that trees and people are often interchanged in Scripture. The righteous flourish *as the palm tree* (Psalm 92:12), the believer is *like a green olive tree in the house of God* (Psalm 52:8), and Gentile believers are part of a wild olive tree that has been grafted into the natural olive tree which is Israel (Romans 11:17).

I have always loved trees. As a child, I lived in Westchester

100

County, New York, an area of the United States blessed with an abundance of trees. In the fall, my father, mother, older brother, and I took long walks in the woods. I gathered Japanese lanterns, bittersweet, milkweed pods, leaves from the giant sugar maples, and all kinds of seeds. In the spring we went looking for pussywillows and delighted in the forsythia that began to color the woods. Summer found us walking through the cool, thick foliage on our way to our canoe at the lake where we fished almost every evening at suppertime. In the winter, we had fun brushing snow off leafy boughs as we wandered through the woods on our way to the frozen lakes where we ice skated and fished through the ice.

We also had many trees on our property in Valhalla, New York. There were huge pine trees, pear trees, cherry trees, maple trees, crabapple trees, peach trees, and Macintosh apple trees. I enjoyed them all and climbed most of them, but the Macintosh was my favorite. When my mother couldn't find me around the house, she'd go looking for me in the apple tree. I'd usually be there, reading books. In the fall I'd be eating apples. When I took a break, I'd hang by my knees or my heels from the limbs of the trees. This was pure delight to me. I had a perfect spot to sit in the apple tree. Hidden in leafy boughs, it was cool, even in the summer. No tree compared with that one!

I left my apple tree and ventured out into the world, where I wandered through many woods and forests in this country and across Europe. I found no trees like my apple tree that bore sweet fruit. Some trees bore fruit, but it was bitter. Most had no fruit at all and left me empty and unsatisfied.

Then, when I was 26-years-old, I found that apple tree again—in Jesus, the Messiah—and my search was over. I found in *Yeshua* the source of great delight, my portion forever. I had known a lot of love in my life, but I found the "greatest love" of all. I embraced the One who alone gives life, nourishes, refreshes, and satisfies the deepest longings of the heart.

There is no god like our God.
There is no beloved like our Beloved.
He longs to be your source of nourishment and refreshing today!

Day 49

...I sat down under His shadow with great delight...
Song of Songs 2:3

Sitting down under the *shadow* of the Beloved refers to the Bride's submission to His authority. She welcomes His protection and the rest she finds in Him. It is a wonderful joy to find rest for one's soul. This verse brings to mind the comforting invitation of *Yeshua* found in Matthew 11:28-30: *"Come to me, all you who labor and are heavy laden, and I will give you rest. Take my yoke upon you and learn from me, for I am gentle and lowly in heart, and you will find rest for your souls. For My yoke is easy and My burden is light."*

Everyone sits under some type of *shadow.* We're all serving somebody. At one time we were servants of sin. In *Yeshua* we become "slaves of righteousness." We are yoked to Him. It is an easy yoke because our Master is the Lord of Heaven and earth. We are yoked to Love itself. Our calling is to follow One who is far stronger, wiser, and more loving than we as He leads the way.

Sometimes we pull back from *Yeshua's* easy yoke and choose another way. A parable in the book of Judges chapter 9 illustrates this truth. The trees went forth to anoint a king over them. First they asked the olive tree to reign over them. When he said no, they asked the fig tree. When he said no, they asked the vine. When he said no, the trees submitted themselves to the bramble (thorn bush). The Bible tells us that they put their trust in his *shadow.*

We can choose under whose *shadow* we sit. The Lord's *shadow* is the only choice that brings great delight. Israel found that out the hard way. Instead of God as their King, they chose Saul. Misery followed. Sometimes we do the same thing. When God isn't the King we want Him to be or think that He should be, we submit ourselves to the bramble.

The apple tree is the better way. The psalmist said: *"Oh taste and see that the Lord is good; blessed is the man who trusts in him!"* (Psalm 34:8). King David had more to say throughout the Book of Psalms about hiding, trusting, and abiding in the *shadow* of the Almighty. We must rejoice in *the shadow of His wings.* God can be trusted!

A *shadow* is a welcome place of refuge. While the Bible has a lot to say about *the shadow of death,* it also shows us the *"shadow* of life" — *Yeshua's shadow.* This *shadow,* spoken of in Psalm 91:1, is called *"the shadow of the Almighty."* It is referring to a secret place of security. The economy may fail, the earth may quake, disasters may surround us on every side, but *"He who dwells in the secret place of the Most High shall abide under the shadow of the Almighty."* That's where I want to be. That's where each of us *can* be, by trusting *Yeshua* with all our heart. Our real life — the life that counts for eternity — is hidden with the Messiah in God.

I remember singing about this deep truth to a group of my kindergarten students and their mothers at an end-of-the-year party at our home many years ago. I shared a song I had written, *"My Life is Hid With the Messiah,"* in an effort to explain to them the motivating force in my life. I often wondered if anyone understood the words. If they didn't, I know that they felt my heart. The words to the chorus become more meaningful to me with each passing year:

But as for me the love that shows
The good I do, is just the glow
From my communion with Jesus my Lord.
In Him the living waters flow.
In Him I live and move and grow.
My life is hidden with Jesus my Lord!

Yeshua's shadow. I love it! It's not *He,* but it's part of Him. Just as Peter Pan, in the traditional children's fairy tale, rejoiced greatly to find the shadow he had lost, I rejoice to see the "shadows" of *Yeshua* in the Old Covenant Scriptures. For instance, the Sabbath is a glorious type of our rest in *Yeshua;* Passover foreshadows The Lamb and His eternal redemption; the Feast of Trumpets looks ahead to the return of Messiah and the final shofar sound. The ancient Jewish marriage customs are shadows of *Yeshua* seeking, selecting, and taking a bride for Himself. The list goes on and on.

Types and shadows add a fullness to our faith. Believers in Jesus, such as former Methodists like myself, who embrace their Jewish roots which include the types and shadows of the Old Testament, will be greatly enriched in the faith.

Our children are always delighted with how big their shadows make them look. Embrace "the body" — *Yeshua* (Colossians 2:16-17) — but don't throw out *the shadow.* It magnifies our precious Lord!

Day 50

...his fruit was sweet to my taste.
Song of Songs 2:3

Traditional Jewish commentators see verse 3 as referring to the twelve months that Israel spent before Mount Sinai feasting on the words of the Torah. *His fruit*, then, refers to the Word of God. Is God's Word sweet? Yes, indeed. Sweeter than honey! We read in Psalm 19:10 that the Word of God is *sweeter than honey and the honeycomb.*

This has been my experience with the Word of God since before I met the Messiah. When the Holy Spirit was wooing me in 1972, I experienced a special sense of well-being and joy when I read the words of the New Testament. The "red letter" passages, spoken by the Messiah Himself, especially touched a chord deep within my soul. I was not yet a "believer," but I sensed a supernatural power tugging at my heart. It was very exciting and sweet!

The day I prayed in my bedroom to accept Yeshua as my Savior and Lord, I began to consume the Holy Scriptures. In fact, in the three days it took us to drive from Bethpage, Long Island, New York, to Fort Lauderdale, Florida, I devoured most of the New Testament. My Jewish husband watched me from behind the wheel of the car as I pored over the pages, hour after hour. Never had I read sweeter words. My joy was full. I found complete satisfaction in the Lover of my soul. Certain passages of the Bible seemed to jump off the pages at me. One of these "kisses" from God continues to shape my life on a daily basis. It is found in the Gospel of John, chapter 15, verse 16: *"You did not choose Me, but I chose you and appointed you that you should go and bear fruit, and that your fruit should remain, that whatever you ask the Father in My name He may give you."*

These words have always been sweet *fruit* to me because they impart a deep knowledge of the election of God, the purpose of God, and the provision of God in my life. God wants to kiss *you* with these words today. He has chosen *you*. He has a great purpose for *your* life. *You* will bear lasting *fruit* through Him. God, your Father, longs to give to you in *Yeshua*'s name!

Messiah has other *fruit* to give us also: the *Fruit* of the Spirit, as outlined in Galatians 5:22-23: "...*love, joy, peace, long suffering, kindness, goodness, faithfulness, gentleness, (and) self-control...*" He wants us to partake of this delicious fruit. As we sit together with Him *in heavenly places* (see Ephesians 2:6), it is as if we were back in the Garden of Eden before the fall. But this time, there's a different tree, and the Lord says, "Eat the fruit!"

This *fruit*—Messiah's *fruit*—must become a part of our own lives. This should be our goal as believers. Neil and I have always believed that *fruit* should be first, and gifts second, in our own walk with the Lord. Character is more important than charisma. This is one of the reasons we try to spend a little time each year among our Mennonite friends in Lancaster County, Pennsylvania. We see luscious *fruit* in their lives, and we desire to expose ourselves and our children to their example.

Fruit naturally develops on a branch that is on a *fruit* tree. *Yeshua* is the *fruit* tree. When you are "in Him" daily, in His Word, yielded to His Spirit, willing to die to all that is unfruitful, you *will* see His *fruit* developing in you. Every time you control your temper, refrain from saying something unkind, bear patiently with a child or someone slower or weaker than yourself, your *fruit* is showing and growing.

Are you experiencing stress? An agricultural discovery was made in Israel not too long ago which showed that plants under stress produce more and sweeter tasting *fruit*. In God, even stress can be good!

Pray with me:

Lord, I desire to bear sweet, lasting fruit for Your Kingdom, starting TODAY. Teach me to love the way You love. Fill me with Your joy and Your perfect peace. Help me to see the fruit that is developing in my life. Make Your Word sweeter than honey to me.

In Yeshua's Name,
Amen!

Day 51

He brought me to the banqueting house...
Song of Songs 2:4

Submission, rest, and trust in Messiah are the doorways to even greater delights. The Bridegroom brings the Shulamite maiden to His *banqueting house. The banqueting house,* in Hebrew, *Beth HaYayin,* literally means *The House of Wine.* Wine in the Scriptures often symbolizes joy, and it is in *the banqueting house* that the first two fruits of the *Ruach HaKodesh*—LOVE and JOY—are made real to the Bride.

Yeshua had a lot to say about joy right before His death. We read the following words in John 15:11: *"These things I have spoken to you, that My joy may remain in you, and that your joy may be full."* What things? The Messiah was speaking about abiding. We are to abide in Him and in His love. His words are to abide in us. That is the gateway into fullness of JOY. I wish I could say that there are no conditions to joy that remains, but that wouldn't be true or faithful to the Words of Scripture. We have joy *if* we abide in the Beloved.

In these last days, the Father is giving many believers a taste of His joy. It's "the wine of His Spirit" that comes as a surprise and manifests itself in holy laughter. I believe that this experience is real and certainly uplifting to those who partake of it. However, I don't believe the joy will last unless the believer's life conforms to the stipulations found in John 15.

As a brand new believer, the Lord sovereignly brought my husband and me to a very special *banqueting house* where we consistently experienced the joy of the Lord. We had been in Florida about one month and were looking for a place where I could be immersed in the ocean. I had an overwhelming desire to follow *Yeshua* in the waters of baptism.

Why the ocean? I love the ocean and I figured that it would be better to have my sins washed away in the ocean than to leave them at the bottom of someone's swimming pool! My husband was so good about going along with me on this. As our search for the "right place" continued, Neil found an article in the newspaper that had a picture of people running through the waves on Fort Lauderdale beach. The caption read: "The Church is growing. Praise the Lord!" Neil said he thought this might be the place for me. We went that night, having no idea what kind of a place we were going to.

When we got there, everyone began to sing, and my husband began to cry. The Spirit of God arrested him in a powerful way. At the end of the service, as new wine flowed from on High, I rushed forward to publicly confess Jesus as my Lord. The minister who prayed with me asked if I had any other requests. I asked him to pray with me that my Jewish husband would commit his life to *Yeshua* also. At that moment I saw Neil on the other side of the church at the altar praying to receive Jesus as his Messiah. He had a vision of *Yeshua* that evening. He was about nine feet tall and said to Neil: "Welcome home, my son. I would have waited another two thousand years for you. Welcome home!"

What a *banqueting house* we had been led to! It was a Pentecostal, Assembly of God church. The minister moved in the gifts of healing and miracles. We knew nothing about life in the Spirit. We just knew we wanted everything God had for us. We were hungry. We were thirsty. We desired God! And He met us there. For almost four years we feasted on the Living Word and drank from Messiah's river of delight. We tasted and saw that the Lord is good! We were never ashamed to go to the altar when an altar call was given. We always needed more of *Yeshua*. It was in that first *banqueting house* that we learned to feed ourselves. The anointing, spoken of in 1 John 2:27, became our teacher. We will be forever grateful to Pastor and Mrs. George Miller for taking us under their wings and teaching us about our Messiah.

Are you hungry and thirsty for more of God? He will lead you to a *banqueting house* where you will experience fullness of joy, satisfaction in Him, and the refreshing new wine of the *Ruach HaKodesh*. The Spirit of God is moving in a new way today crossing denominational lines and drawing God's people closer to Himself. *Yeshua* is preparing His Bride.

We don't have to strive to find God's best for us because our God always takes the initiative. *He* brings His Bride to the *banqueting house*. This is masculinity taking the initiative. I love what C.S. Lewis said in reference to this: "God is *so* masculine that all of creation is feminine by comparison."

Believe God to bring joy into your life as you abide in Him. Praise Him — by faith — for bringing you to the *banqueting house*.

Day 52

...his banner over me was love.
Song of Songs 2:4

The feast that takes place in the *banqueting house* is first and foremost a *LOVE* FEAST. The revelation of the love of God is the greatest revelation a soul will ever receive. The Bride of Messiah finds the reason for her very being in this revealed truth.

Messiah is all *Love,* even when He leads us in paths of chastening and correction, even when we suffer. He is still *Love.* This *love* is like a *banner over us.* This word *banner,* in Hebrew, is *degel,* which can also mean *a flag or a standard. Love* is what the Bride of Messiah rallies around. *Love* is our highest goal. *Love* is *Yeshua's* victory *banner.* And as the little chorus says: *"Love is a flag flown high from the castle of my heart, when the King is in residence there!"*

Yeshua's love covers the "bridal-soul." Another way of picturing this covering rather than as a flag would be as a *chuppah* or wedding canopy under which a Jewish couple stand as they declare their wedding vows. This canopy of *love* covers both bride and groom. The "bridal-soul" cries out, like Ruth in the Bible: *"...spread the corner of your garment over me, since you are a kinsman-redeemer"* (Ruth 3:9 NIV). That is precisely what Messiah has done for us. While we were yet exposed to sin's scorching rays, *Yeshua* provided a covering for us. Proverbs 10:12 tells us that *"Love covers all sins."* Forgiving *love,* restoring *love,* redeeming *love,* unconditional *love.* This is the Messiah's *banner* over each "bridal-soul."

Once redeemed, *Yeshua's* Bride continues under His *banner of love.* Since God Himself is *Love,* our life in His Son is to be a life of immersion in the *love* of God. In *love* we must live, in *love* we must *move,* in *love* we must have our being. What a high calling! What a challenge to each of us, since in order to love we must put self last and God and others first! He will help us as we determine to walk in *love.* As Jude admonished in his New Covenant epistle: *"...keep yourselves in the love of God..."* (Jude 21).

Self-control enters here. When we are hurt, offended, slighted, passed over, attacked, or misunderstood, our natural tendency is to step out of the *love* of God. The flesh is pleased when we retaliate, seek vengeance, speak evil of someone, or act unkindly. But God is not pleased. *He* must be our primary concern. The Lord is worthy of our noblest, our best, our total abandonment to Him.

Reminders of His great *love,* such as the following one spoken to my heart by the Lord on August 3, 1976, help keep me focused on His *love* as my *banner,* and my goal in life: "As the rivers flow to the sea, so does My love flow to My children who seek Me and acknowledge Me in all their ways. Yea, I love with a love everlasting, and I ask nothing in return but obedience. My standards are different from yours. The sweat of your brow does not move Me, but your faith does. All the necessary sacrificing has been done by My Son. Rejoice in this burden being lifted from you. Yours is not to sorrow, but to rejoice in such love."

Rejoice in the love of our King today. Accept by faith the truth of His *banner of love* covering you. Because He *loves* you, you can *love* others. You have been set free to be an emissary of the *love* of God! *Love* will be YOUR victory *banner!*

*L*ife
*O*f
*V*ictory
*E*veryday

LOVE *is the way!*

Day 53

Stay me with flagons, comfort me with apples: for I am sick of love. Song of Songs 2:5

Have you ever been *love-sick*? Have you ever written love poems or letters to someone you loved who was far from you? When my mother died, I found a box of love letters that my father had written to her while he was in the army. She had saved them for over forty years. Now I have them and will probably save them for another forty. I also found a love poem that I had written in college, at least five years before I met the Lover of my soul. I'll never forget two lines of that poem because they are so unusual:

Do you love someone dearly whom you've never met?
Do you inwardly shine like a jewel?

God was drawing me to Himself years before I was aware of it. He's been *love-sick* for you and me since time began — longing for the day when we would say yes to Him, looking forward to the day when we will be conformed to the image of His Son. Just as God is love-sick for us, we need to be love-sick for Him.

According to Rambam, a revered Jewish philosopher, proper love for God is loving Him and being "constantly enraptured by Him like a *love-sick* individual, whose mind is at no time free from his passion for a particular woman, the thought of her filling his heart at all times; when sitting down or rising up, when eating or drinking."

Metzudas David, another famous Jewish scholar, expressed *love-sickness* in this way: "My soul swoons for the return of the *Shechinah* [the glory or manifest presence of God]."

As young believers, we experienced this passion. My husband and I were at our home congregation every time the doors were open. We never missed a service unless we were very ill. We couldn't get enough of the Bible, the Spirit, or the Beloved. We wanted more and more of Jesus. We were indeed *love-sick*.

Our Messiah, who is also the great Physician, has the cure for *love-sickness*: His presence, more of Himself. He strengthens and comforts us with His sweet fruit.

Flagons are dainties or raisin cakes. I like to call them Holy Spirit iron! *Apples*, as we've already seen, are the fruit from the Apple Tree: *Yeshua*, the Messiah. When the original "bridal-souls," the apostles, faced the departure of the Bridegroom, *Yeshua* comforted them by explaining that in their *love-sickness,* He would come to them: *"And I will pray the Father, and he shall give you another Comforter, that he may abide with you for ever;" "I will not leave you comfortless: I will come to you"* (John 14:16,18 KJV).

This same Comforter, the *Ruach HaKodesh*, or Holy Spirit, comes today to each "bridal-soul" in the Body of Messiah. He dwells *with* us and is *in* us. It is the *Ruach HaKodesh* who teaches the Bride about her Bridegroom. I remember a time in my life, perhaps ten years after meeting the Messiah, when the *Ruach HaKodesh* spoke to my heart (kissed me) a number of times and said, "Let me show you something new and special about *Yeshua*." Then He'd reveal some aspect of *Yeshua*'s character, and I'd meditate on it. One time it was His strength, another time His compassion, another His love of music. The Holy Spirit does not seek to draw attention to Himself. He longs to minister to the *love-sick* Bride who is only satisfied with more of the Beloved. The Spirit makes the Beloved real to us.

Sometimes we sense an emptiness, a spiritual dryness, and don't realize that the only thing that can satisfy this need is more of God. We try to fill the void, to comfort ourselves, with other things. For some people, food becomes the major source of comfort. For others, male-female relationships. Others find comfort in building a home, pursuing a career, or achieving success on the job.

The Hebrew word used for *comfort* in this verse is *raphad*, which is a primary root that literally means *to make a bed*. The implication here is intimacy. The only answer for *love-sickness* is union with the Beloved. *Raphad* also implies *refreshing*. There's nothing like a new awareness of the love of God to refresh the soul.

> *Lord, help us to seek comfort in You.*
> *We desire greater intimacy with our Messiah Yeshua.*
> *Holy Spirit, make Him more real to us today.*
> *AMEN!*

Day 54

*His left hand is under my head, and his right hand
doth embrace me.*   Song of Songs 2:6

The Bride in this verse is in wonderful union and communion with the Beloved. She is in His tender *embrace*. How
each of us longs to be *embraced*! We need a touch from someone, especially from our God. How does the Lord *embrace*
His own? Where are His arms today? His Bride is His hand
extended and His open arms. *We* need to *embrace* others.

Touch is crucial from infancy on. Many studies have been
conducted on the importance of touch to healthy physical
and emotional development. Infants who are never touched
and cuddled often become sick. Some die. People need to be
touched as an expression of love. In our marriage seminars,
we always mention the study that showed that women
need eight to ten hugs or touches per day from someone
significant in their lives in order to maintain good physical
and emotional health. Hugging is definitely healthy!

Touching, giving "holy hugs," is also an important
ministry in the Body of Messiah. Those who live alone,
single parents, widows, and widowers especially need hugs
from the Bride. Do you need a hug? Hug someone else, and
you'll get one back!

There is a spiritual *embrace* which is almost as real as the
physical one. I have experienced this many times. It happens
during times of deep worship. There's an awareness of
God's manifest presence. A loving tenderness is perceived
in the Spirit! The Glory of God becomes a reality. *Yeshua's*
Bride senses the same care and protection at that moment
that a baby feels when his mother gently supports his little
head and cradles him in her arms.

I remember the first time I held my oldest son Jonathan

in my arms. I was totally inexperienced with babies, never having baby-sat or had younger brothers or sisters as a child. I actually was somewhat afraid of babies. I was sure they were very, very fragile. The hospital nurse showed me how to put my arm under Jonathan's head to support it. I soon felt comfortable holding him. And never, ever, did I drop him! The same is true of God. He never lets go. He never drops His Bride. She is secure in His *embrace*.

Those who really belong to *Yeshua* have been a gift to Him from His Father. They are His forever. Their love relationship will only intensify after death when the *embrace* will be so much more real. I love the reference to the *hand* of God in John 10:28-29. *Yeshua* is speaking to His disciples about His sheep: *"And I give them eternal life, and they shall never perish; neither shall anyone snatch them out of My hand. My Father, who has given them to Me, is greater than all; and no one is able to snatch them out of My Father's hand."*

Nothing and no one can separate us from the love of God which is ours in the Messiah, *Yeshua*. He's holding us tight. When we are at our weakest, He is there to sustain and support us.

Some early commentators of The Song have pointed out that the left *hand* of God, the one that supports us, is not always obvious to the "bridal-soul." It is "His *hand* upon us for good" that keeps us from danger when we are unaware that danger even exists. It is the *hand* that cradles us while we sleep and arranges circumstances on our behalf. In contrast, the *right hand* is the one which represents God's dealings, the working out of His will in the life of His Bride. The *right hand* is the one we would say "Stop!" to in those moments when we feel pain, heat, or pressure, as *Yeshua* shapes and molds us in the perfecting process. However, we must yield to His righteous *right hand* because all God's dealings with us spring forth from His love.

Don't shrink back from His touch. His *hands*, carpenter's *hands*, may be a little rough, but they are strong and they forever bear marks of love for me and for you.

Rest in *Yeshua's embrace*, and then touch others for Him.

$\mathcal{D}ay$ 55

*I charge you, O ye daughters of Jerusalem, by
the roes, and by the hinds of the field, that ye
stir not up, nor awake my love, till he please.*

Song of Songs 2:7

Timing is important in the Kingdom of God! Even good
works done in *Yeshua's* Name are sometimes less effective
spiritually than they should be because God's timing is
missed. Ecclesiastes 3:1 says that there is *a time and a season
for everything.* Verse 5 even says that there is *a time to embrace*
and *a time to refrain from embracing.*

The Bride, in this verse from The Song, is asking *the
daughters of Jerusalem* to refrain from disturbing the embrace,
the rest, the union, the intimate communion that the Bride is
having with her Beloved. It is not time to move on yet. The
Bride is not ready for the next step. God is at work. His Holy
Spirit has a sign hung out that says: "Do not disturb!" Can
the daughters read it? Will they heed the admonition?

By the roes and by the hinds of the field is an oath that is used
to emphasize the seriousness and urgency of the request.
It is used twice in The Song: in 2:7 and 3:5. Each time, *the
daughters of Jerusalem* are adjured not to hasten what God is
doing.

"Wait on the Lord." This is the message of verse 7. *His*
timing is perfect. He's not in a hurry. (*We* usually are). *He's*
got all the time in the world. (*We* usually don't).

The verse brings to my mind the beautiful, quiet deer
that inhabited the woods near my childhood home in
Westchester County, New York. I'll never forget the day my
dad took me deer hunting with him and, instead of going
into the woods with him, I decided to wait in the car. I was
about eleven-years-old. After a couple of hours, I looked up

and, right in front of me, stood about eight huge deer. They stared at me as they silently and swiftly crossed the road into the woods on the other side. I was speechless.

A short while later, my dad returned to the car. He was upset that he hadn't seen even one deer. I told him that they'd been to see me! He made some kind of oath about *roes and hinds of the field*, and I was secretly glad that his bow and arrow had missed the majestic creatures.

Our souls need times of stillness. There are times when we pant after the living water, longing after the Lord, seeking only to stay in His presence. When we are there, we should be reluctant to run off. We are often in danger of grieving God's Holy Spirit when we pray and jump up to go somewhere before God has a chance to answer. We watch the clock, or the schedule, or the bulletin in worship services, and don't allow God the time to do the deep work He desires to do in our hearts.

Love can't be rushed. We can't *make* our loved ones love the Lord. We can't *force* our friends and neighbors to accept Messiah. We *can* pray for the Holy Spirit to have *His* way in their lives, and we *can* make room for Him to work.

Well-meaning people can sometimes pressure us to move faster or to do something that God is not asking us to do. Stand firm. Please the Lord. Speak the truth in love and humility, resist the "fear of man," and fear God.

We need to be sensitive to God's timing and leading in our lives. He is with us. He is working in each of us, perfecting His Bride. Let us seek to please Him, to walk softly before Him, and to welcome the work of His Spirit in our lives.

$\mathcal{D}ay$ 56

The voice of my beloved!   Song of Songs 2:8

The voice of my Beloved, kol Dodi in Hebrew, has been a major theme of my life since the day I met *Yeshua*. This is not something that originated in my heart but, I believe, in the heart of God for His purposes and His glory.

The Spirit of God gently, but powerfully, wooed me for most of a year from 1972 to 1973. I began reading the New Covenant Scriptures, and the words printed in red (the words of Messiah) burned into my soul. I could sense God speaking to me. I was not yet His child, but still He spoke!

When I finally prayed to receive Jesus on July 25, 1973, in my bedroom in Bethpage, New York, the desire to hear God's voice was already firmly rooted in my heart. I knelt by our bed with Neil watching and opened up a little *Four Spiritual Laws* booklet that my friend Cathy had given me. She had told me to pray from it when I was ready, and I was ready! Tears streamed down my cheeks as I confessed my sin, my separation from God, my self-directed life, and my desire to place Yeshua on the throne of my heart.

After concluding the prayer in the booklet, I continued on my own. I told *Yeshua* that now that we had settled the basic question of to whom I belonged, I was ready to receive some miracles! I asked for 3: (1) To never smoke again (I had tried to quit on our honeymoon and had such terrible withdrawal symptoms that it almost ruined the marriage!) (2) To never drink again (There was alcoholism on my father's side of the family) and (3) To always hear the voice of God. God began to answer each of these three requests immediately.

My prayer concerning *the voice of the Beloved* had to be Spirit led. I was not attending a church. No one had taught

121

me about God's voice. But I had already had a taste of the sweet communion with God that is promised to those who are in Messiah. I wanted — passionately desired — that voice to be a part of my life forever.

For many people, hearing the voice of God is not something that happens today. Jewish people particularly have a hard time with this concept. They see God as holy, awesome, and, for the most part, distant. His Name is considered too sacred to write in its entirety; so, instead of God, most religious Jews write G-d. Not too long ago I read an article in a local Jewish newspaper in which three rabbis addressed the question: "Does G-d talk to me, like he spoke to Moses?" (The Bible tells us, in Exodus 33:11, that God spoke to Moses *"face to face, as a man speaks to his friend."*)

The first rabbi said that just as he was not sure exactly how G-d communicated with Moses, neither was he sure how G-d can or will really communicate with any of us.

The second rabbi stated that, thus far, he had not experienced a "direct transmission" from G-d, and if it were to happen, he was not sure that he could be able to survive the intensity of a direct revelation. He also mentioned that the "Rabbis" have taught that the age of prophecy has ceased and that G-d no longer reveals himself to mankind in a direct manner.

The third rabbi said that the Torah itself proclaims that the unmediated, face-to-face, prophetic relationship which Moses shared with God was only for him. He went on to make a valid statement about the Word of God: "...the Torah has become the oracle by which Israel's scholars and people can infer G-d's will and apply it to our lives."

Yes, God does speak through His Word. He kisses His people with the kisses of His mouth. But there is more. In the Torah itself, in Deuteronomy 18:18, God tells us about a new prophet like Moses, who will be God's mouthpiece — His voice: *"I will raise up for them a Prophet like you [Moses] from among their brethren, and will put My words in His mouth, and He shall speak to them all that I command Him."*

The Prophet like Moses is *Yeshua*! Not only did God

speak to Him face-to-face, but His voice and God's voice have become one because *Yeshua* and the Father are one. When *Yeshua* speaks, we hear directly from God. Thank God that He still speaks today!

Day 57

*My sheep hear My voice, and I know them, and
they follow Me.*   John 10:27

This magnificent proclamation/promise from the mouth
of *Yeshua*, our Shepherd/King, was made at the Jewish
Feast of Dedication (*Hanukkah*, in Hebrew). The main point
is very clear: *Yeshua*'s sheep hear His voice! This is part of
their inheritance in Him. Yet, so many of God's sheep have
been robbed of this precious inheritance. John 10 has a lot to
say about *the Good Shepherd*, His *sheep*, and *His voice*. It also
talks about *the thief*.

Let's meditate today on a few of *Yeshua*'s statements as
found in John chapter 10: *"... he calls his own sheep by name
and leads them out"* (verse 3). *"...I am the door of the sheep. All
who ever came before me are thieves and robbers, but the sheep did
not hear them. I am the door. If anyone enters by Me, he will be
saved, and will go in and out and find pasture. The thief does not
come except to steal, and to kill, and to destroy. I have come that
they may have life, and that they may have it more abundantly"*
(verses 7-10).

A key to the abundant life that Jesus promised is hearing
His voice! The enemy of *Yeshua*, *hasatan* in Hebrew, literally
the accuser, is interested in keeping believers from hearing
the voice of God. No awareness of God's voice: no two-way
communication; no real relationship; spiritual bankruptcy.

God continues to speak, but our ability to hear, to tune in
to His Voice, is the battleground. The world is full of noise
and voices, and many of the voices clamor for our attention.
I'm reminded of the year I had twenty-seven students in
my kindergarten class and no aide. When I introduced
something new, the children were given instructions and
sent to their seats to begin working. I would inevitably hear

at least twelve voices shouting "Teacher!" "Mrs. Lash!" all at once. They all needed my help—immediately!

I actually loved all those little voices and the furious pace of meeting each need, but the Lord couldn't get through to me the way He wanted to. He was jealous. One day during "quiet time" as the children were on their rest mats, He spoke to me and said, "I'm calling you out of kindergarten teaching." I silently mourned the end of my musical and dramatic productions, cooking extravaganzas, exciting units of study, and, most of all, those adoring faces that delighted to listen to my voice and hated it when Friday came. Still, I made my decision to follow my Shepherd.

My teaching job—my students—had crowded out God's voice from my life. The thief had subtly gotten me distracted with something beautiful and good, even godly, but nevertheless no longer in the will of God—for me.

Hearing God's voice takes time and quiet. Listening must be cultivated as a communication skill. There must be desire, and hearing God's voice must be a priority.

God wants *you* to hear His voice. He knows you, and knows what gets in the way of your hearing His voice. Tune in today so that He can reveal any distractions in your life and tell you what to do about them.

Yeshua continued, in John 10:16, by saying something about His voice that many people over the years have misunderstood: *"And other sheep I have which are not of this fold; them also I must bring, and they will hear My voice; and there will be one flock and one shepherd."*

Yeshua was not speaking to gentiles here. He was talking to His fellow Jews. The *other sheep* are the non-Jews who will be joined to the House of Israel: Jew and non-Jew together; one flock; one shepherd; and *one voice* that unites them.

Pray with me:

Lord, I want to hear your voice! I am one of Your sheep. I belong to you. Speak to me and open my spiritual ears to hear what You are saying. Then give me the grace, the power, and the determination to obey and to follow you.
In Yeshua's Name, **AMEN**

Day 58

The voice of the Lord is upon the waters...
Psalm 29:3

The Lord wants us to continue to meditate on His *voice*! Psalm 29 is a good vehicle for this. The entire Psalm speaks about *the voice of the Lord*. It tells us that *the voice of the Lord* is powerful and full of majesty. *The voice of the Lord breaks the cedars, divides the flames of fire,* and *shakes the wilderness. The voice of the Lord makes the deer give birth* and *strips the forest bare.*

What does *the voice of the Lord* sound like? I discussed this question with the children of Sar Shalom Hebrew Academy (our Temple's school) in December of 1994 at a chapel service. The children seemed genuinely interested in knowing more about the *voice* of God. I told them that many times God's *voice* sounds like our own voice. That's why some believers don't know when God is speaking to them. They say: "That's just me!" It could be. Or, it could be God. It takes time, experience, practice, knowledge of God's Word, and faith to accurately discern whose *voice* you are hearing. There will be mistakes. I can almost guarantee that! But they are part of the learning process and should not be a source of discouragement.

God's *voice* will always agree with His Word and will never contradict it. God's *voice* may be convicting, but it won't be condemning. God's *voice* may sound like yours, but it will be borne on the wings of the Spirit. Its message will be Heaven-sent, not something you came up with.

The *still, small voice* spoken of in 1 Kings 19:12 is sometimes hard to recognize. But God doesn't generally speak to His children in the wind, the earthquake, or the fire. He speaks in a delicate, whisper-like *voice*. To hear *the still, small voice,* your mind and your spirit must be still!

I waited to hear that *still, small voice* on July 25, 1979, my sixth born-again birthday in *Yeshua*. We lived near the ocean at the time, and I went to the beach with my little beach chair to talk to the Lord early in the morning before the crowds came. I opened up our conversation with: "Lord, Your Word says that Your *voice* is *over the waters*. I believe that. Since it's my born-again birthday today and I know how much You like to give presents, I'd like a gift from You — something worthy of Your great creativity that will bear much fruit for Your Kingdom. And I'm not going home until I receive it!"

I sat near the water's edge for a while, digging my toes in the sand and admiring the sparkling white lucina shells that adorn Fort Lauderdale beach. Then I began to hum a song I'd recently heard based on Ecclesiastes 11:1:

> *You gotta cast your bread upon the waters,*
> *And it will come back home on every wave* .... .

Over and over the words to Ecclesiastes 11:1 worked into my Spirit. "The Word of God is the bread of life," I mused: "How can I cast God's Word into the waters?" Then I knew, "The shells!" I've collected seashells since I was a toddler. When Neil married me, he had to agree to take all my cardboard boxes of seashells, too!

The lucinas were smooth, perfect to write on. That was it! I knew I was to write messages from God on the shells and cast them out into the waters. Neil suggested that I put our phone number on the inside of each shell so that sincere seekers could have someone to contact.

I found that Sharpie permanent markers and Krylon acrylic spray were the best combination for the lucinas and I began to make message-shells. When the ocean was rough, I threw the shells on the sand near the water's edge so that people walking along the beach would find them.

God's Spirit had spoken to me through His *still, small voice*. One kiss from Ecclesiastes 11:1 has led to hundreds of people hearing the voice of God. The stories of people who have found my little white lucina shells over the years would fill an entire book.

God's *voice* can be heard in other ways, too. He speaks through circumstances. He speaks through other people. And, of course, He speaks through His Word — His love letter to each one of us.

Are you hungry to hear *the voice* of God? I hope so!

Prepare your heart to listen. Expect a kiss.

You *will* hear *the voice of the Beloved!*

$\mathcal{D}ay$ 59

...behold, he cometh...   Song of Songs 2:8

This is a promise. *He is coming!* The Beloved will not remain far off. His voice often precedes His coming. We see an example of this throughout the pages of the *Tanach*. The voice of the Messiah proclaims the glorious truth that God's plan to send a Redeemer to Israel will be realized *in the fullness of time.* Three verses in Psalm 40:6-8 are alive with the sound of the voice of Messiah: *"Sacrifice and offering You did not desire; My ears You have opened: Burnt offering and sin offering You did not require. Then I said, 'Behold, I come; in the scroll of the Book it is written of me. I delight to do Your will, O my God, and Your law is within my heart.'"*

This is *Yeshua* the Messiah speaking before He actually came to earth to carry out His Father's plan. We hear His voice again in Isaiah 61:1, as *Yeshua* proclaims His divine mission: *"The Spirit of the Lord God is upon Me, because the LORD has anointed Me to preach good tidings to the poor; He has sent me to heal the brokenhearted, to proclaim liberty to the captives, and the opening of the prison to those who are bound."*

First His voice, then His coming. He is speaking to us today by His Holy Spirit. And He is coming again! One Messiah; two comings. This truth has been hidden from the Jewish people for hundreds of years, but many are seeing it now. The Lord is speaking to the hearts of Jewish people all over the world, revealing Jesus to them. Thousands of Russian Jews are receiving the Lord. God's voice is calling many of His people home to Israel. Prophecy is being fulfilled on a daily basis. God is speaking! Messiah is coming — again.

The word *behold,* in Hebrew, is *hineh (prounounced HEE-nay).*

129

It implies *seeing. Look! Behold! See!* We see with eyes of faith. Our Bridegroom King is coming for us. He promised that He would in John 14:3 when He said, *"And if I go and prepare a place for you, I will come again and receive you to Myself; that where I am, there you may be also."*

God's Holy Spirit is preparing a Bride for that day. *"And the Spirit and the Bride say, 'Come'!"* to all those who haven't yet met the Beloved because time is running out (Revelation 22:17). *Yeshua,* speaking through the pages of the Bible, in Revelation 22:12, assures us of this: *"And behold, I am coming quickly, and My reward is with Me…"*

What about today? Is *Yeshua* coming to us where we live and work, where we deal with so many demands, pressures, expectations, and assignments? Yes! *Behold, He comes!* He has promised to never leave us comfortless. He has promised to never leave us nor forsake us. He comes to us on a daily basis in the person of the Holy Spirit.

I have been very moved in the past 24 hours as I've begun to read a book about the Holy Spirit. I am finding much deep revelation and truth about both the voice of God and His presence in our lives. God is speaking to me to cry out for more of Him, to welcome His Spirit in my home and in all I do.

"Come, Holy Spirit, make my Bridegroom even more real to me! He went away and sent *You* in His place. Please come and be with me right now. I desire sweet communion with You." This was my prayer this morning. I realized for the first time that my hours at the piano worshipping the Lord with either tears of joy or laughter have been times of His coming. *Yeshua,* by the *Ruach HaKodesh,* comes to us where we live.

Welcome the Holy Spirit.
See Him coming by faith.
Make room for Him in your life!

$\mathcal{D}ay$ 60

... leaping upon the mountains, skipping upon the hills.   Song of Songs 2:8

Our Bridegroom King always comes in victory! He is a resurrected Lord! No *mountain* can keep Him away from us. The first time Messiah came, He *leaped* over the *mountains* of sin and condemnation, bringing us salvation. No sin is beyond His saving power. No family situation, no spiritual, mental, or emotional bondage is too great an obstacle for Him. *Yeshua leaped* over them all in bringing redemption to the world.

The prophet Isaiah foretold this great salvation in Isaiah chapter 40:4-5 when he wrote: *"Every valley shall be exalted, and every mountain and hill shall be brought low... The glory of the Lord shall be revealed, and all flesh shall see it together..."* In *Yeshua*, our Heavenly Bridegroom, the Glory of the Lord is revealed!

A number of rabbis have believed over the centuries that this verse from The Song of Songs refers to the Messiah and His redemption. Most have not made a connection, however, between the verse and Jesus of Nazareth. Nevertheless, it speaks of Him. *Yeshua* met a tax collector named Matthew and *leaped* over the vileness of his profession, drawing him into the Kingdom of love and the Master's service. He met a prostitute named Mary and *leaped* over her shame and degradation, transforming an outcast into a "bridal-soul." He met a rich man named Zacchaeus and *leaped* over unrighteousness and a life without purpose, bringing joy and newness of life.

Yeshua skipped over *hills,* as well. He *skipped* over Peter's petulance, Thomas' doubts, James' and John's egos, Martha's busyness, and much more.

There was one *mountain* that seemed as if it had conquered the Lord: Mount Calvary. This *mountain* was the place where the Son of God met with defeat — or so it seemed. He was crucified. Death had defeated Him, but only for a brief moment. *Yeshua leaped* over that *mountain* as well. Death could not hold Him, and He rose from the dead. Death, the highest *mountain*, the fiercest enemy, was trampled over gloriously by *Yeshua*, our Lord and King. Not only death but all principalities and powers are now under His feet.

As we await the second coming of Messiah, we are aware of many *hills* and *mountains* all around us. Sin abounds. Economies fail. Violence erupts on every side. The very earth quakes beneath our feet.

God's Spirit responds to all of this with: "FEAR NOT. YOUR GOD IS IN CONTROL!" He is greater than any *hill* or *mountain*. He *skips*. He *leaps*. He bounds over them effortlessly. For with God, nothing is impossible! One of Neil's favorite verses speaks about Messiah's victory over all the *mountains* of life. It is found in John 16:33: *"...In the world you will have tribulation; but be of good cheer, I have overcome the world."* Rejoice! Don't worry! The victory is the Lord's!

Cast your cares upon Him today. Give Him the *hills*, the disappointments, the setbacks, the frustrations, and the concerns. Give Him the *mountains* as well , whether they be the loss of a job, a loved one, a home, disease, abuse, divorce, or a stronghold of the enemy within your family.

The Messiah's victory is yours! Because He *leaps*, you too can *leap*. Just as He *skips*, you can *skip*. Let Psalm 18:29 be your confession today:

For by You [God] I can run against a troop,
And by my God I can leap over a wall.

$\mathcal{D}ay$ 61

My beloved is like a roe or a young hart...
Song of Songs 2:9

The Bride describes her victorious, saving Lord. He is *like a roe* (gazelle) *or a young hart.* The Hebrew word for *gazelle, tzvee,* comes from a root word meaning *prominence* or *beauty.* It also carries the connotation of *goodly, pleasant, and glorious.* The Hebrew word for *hart, ayal,* comes from a root word meaning *strength* and refers to *a stag or male deer.*

The very nature of *the gazelle* and *the hart* is to leap effortlessly over the roughest heights with great ease. This is the very nature of God's Messiah. He is beautiful in His strength. He is graceful and glorious.

Tzvee, meaning *glorious,* is used a few times in the Holy Scriptures. The promised land is referred to as *glorious* in Ezekiel 20:6, 15 and Daniel 11:16, 41. The temple mount is referred to as the *glorious holy mountain* in Daniel 11:45. The Lord of hosts is prophesied as a future *crown of glory* to the remnant of His people in Isaiah 28:5. The *Branch of the Lord* is called beautiful and glorious in Isaiah 4:2.

This same glory is the glory of the *Shekinah,* the manifest presence of God that rested on *Yeshua* when He walked upon the earth. There was *glory* at His birth as *the glory* of the Lord shone around shepherds and as an angel of the Lord proclaimed *good tidings of great joy!* There was *glory* at *Yeshua's* dedication in the Temple. Simeon said of the child: *"For my eyes have seen your salvation [Yeshua] which You have prepared before the face of all peoples, a light to bring revelation to the Gentiles, and the glory of Your people Israel"* (Luke 2:30-32).

Yeshua came into the world to be *glory* to His own people. The Apostle John had the following to say about the *glory* that accompanied the incarnation: *"And the Word became flesh and dwelt among us, and we beheld His glory, the glory as of the only begotten of the Father, full of grace and truth"* (John 1:14). *Yeshua* had shared that *glory* with His Father before coming to earth. We read in John 17:5 His own words: *"And now, O Father, glorify Me together with Yourself, with the glory which I had with You before the world was."*

The Bible tells us that the first time *Yeshua manifested His glory* was at Cana in Galilee when He performed His first public miracle. This *kiddush* of His ministry was appropriately a "marriage miracle." *Yeshua* turned water into wine at a wedding feast! What was natural became supernatural. What was empty became full. *Yeshua's* disciples saw the *glory,* and they believed in Him (John 2:11).

Our Beloved is glorious. He is *The King of Glory* (Psalm 24:7). The God of Abraham, Isaac, and Jacob has appointed Him heir of all things. Through Him, God made the worlds. God's Son is *the brightness of His [God's] "glory"* and *the express image of His person* (Hebrews 1:2-3). Glory!

Our beloved was faithful to the One who appointed Him, just as Moses was faithful in all His house (Hebrews 3:2). However, *Yeshua* has been counted worthy of more glory than Moses. Moses was a fruitful servant in God's house. *Yeshua* is a Son over God's house (Hebrews 3:2-6). His is the greater glory.

One of the amazing things about our glorious Lord is that He has given His *glory* to each one of us! In His High Priestly prayer of John chapter 17, prayed shortly before His death, *Yeshua* interceded on behalf of those who believed in Him and those who would believe through their words: *"that they all may be one, as You, Father, are in Me, and I in You; that they also may be one in Us, that the world may believe that You sent Me. And the GLORY which You gave Me I have given them, that they may be one just as We are one"* (John 17:21-22).

Join me in prayer today:

> *Lord, show us that glory! Help us to walk in the Spirit and to stand in Your glory. Then we will be able to cross all barriers and truly be One Body, One Bride. Thank you for Your glory in my life!*

Day 62

...behold, he standeth behind our wall, he looketh forth at the windows, shewing himself through the lattice.   Song of Songs 2:9

The concept of God's glory being partially blocked from view is not a new idea in Scripture. Moses said to God, as recorded in Exodus 33:18, *"...Please, show me Your glory."* The Lord told Moses that he could not see God's face, for no man could see Him and live. This was the Lord's solution: *"So it shall be, while My glory passes by, that I will put you in the cleft of the rock, and will cover you with My hand while I pass by. Then I will take away My hand, and you shall see My back; but My face shall not be seen"* (Exodus 33:22-23).

We get glimpses of God's glory. But mostly we *see through a glass dimly.* One day we will see Him *face to face.* We know *in part,* but then we shall know, *just as we are known* (1 Corinthians 13:12).

I've never seen *Yeshua* face to face, but I have had a few visions of Him. One of these occurred at a Sabbath service at our local congregation in Fort Lauderdale in May of 1994. I was worshipping the Lord at the altar, basking in His sweet presence. In my heart there was a desire for more of the Beloved. I was spiritually hungry. God surprised me with His love as He has done so many times in the past, and then I had a fleeting vision of *Yeshua.* He was walking toward me with His arms outstretched, ready to put His arms around me. He said to me: "Let's dance. We've got to start practicing now to get ready for the big day." The vision ended and filled me with the joy that comes from realizing the extent of the Bridegroom's love. I felt holy laughter bubble up from my innermost being.

I didn't see His face. I only saw up to His neck. I focused

on His outstretched arms. Those same arms are extended to each of us today. Oh, how glorious it will be when they embrace us, and we dance with *Yeshua* at the Marriage Supper of the Lamb! (Please don't be offended; they always dance at Jewish weddings!)

But for now, we must realize that He stands gazing at us lovingly, longing to draw closer. Something separates us! Song of Songs 2:9 calls it *our wall*.

The Hebrew word for *wall* here is *kotel*. This is the *only* time the word *kotel* is used in the Holy Scriptures. If you've ever been to Israel you've probably been to a place called the *Kotel*. It's also called the Western Wall and is the only remaining part of the outer wall of the Great Temple in Jerusalem. Many Jewish people believe that when the Temple was destroyed in 70 A.D. the Spirit of God remained behind the Wall.

I believe that today the Spirit of God is asking us to consider if there might be any walls between us and our Bridegroom. There are so many things in the flesh realm that hinder our walk with Him. Busyness is always a wall I have to contend with, confess as a sin, and forsake. Unbelief, self-will, and pride keep *Yeshua* at a distance, as well.

In spite of the walls we put up, our Messiah continues to show Himself to us. He finds cracks in our walls and makes them windows. Verse 9 says that these windows are *lattice-like*. The word *lattice* ministers so much grace to me! God just can't stop loving us. He *must* have some contact with us. He finds an opening and peeks through. He's so patient and long-suffering!

Yeshua longs to show Himself to His Jewish people—to *all* people. Even now, He's showing Himself through *the lattice*. Let's determine to remove all obstacles that separate us from our Lord, knowing that no matter what, He'll still be there for us—with outstretched arms!

Day 63

My beloved spake, and said unto me, Rise up
[arise], my love, my fair one, and come away.
Song of Songs 2:10

The *Beloved*, *Dod* in Hebrew, now beckons to his Bride.
The words he speaks are some of the most beautiful in the
whole Bible. They are sweet to the ear of the child of God.
Rise up, or *arise*, is *koom* in Hebrew, from a primary root
which can also mean *abide, continue, get up, lift up, remain,*
stir up, strengthen, and succeed.

The Messiah is calling His Bride to come higher, to come
apart with him. He desires her! He wants her to separate
herself unto Him. He has more for her to learn. It is time for
a step of faith.

Arise, My Love has deep personal meaning to me. Many
years ago, in the early 1980s, when I first began studying
The Song, I would read from chapter 2 and then spend
time worshipping the Lord at the piano. One day while
meditating on the phrase *"Arise, My Love,"* the Lord began
to give me a song, both lyrics and melody at once. For
nearly two hours, I was *caught up in the Spirit* with Him.

When the anointing lifted, I had written an entire song
and sensed that *Yeshua* Himself had sung it to me. This has
only happened to me once in my life. I've written other
songs, moved by the Holy Spirit, but this was different.
Yeshua sang this particular song into existence.

Our good friend Jonathan Settel recorded *"Arise, My*
Love" in a somewhat updated jazzier version than I heard
it that day. Nevertheless, I am thrilled to hear his voice
singing the words sung to me by *Yeshua*. Perhaps we'll all
hear our Messiah utter the words *Arise, My Love* on the day
He comes to catch us away.

Even Jewish commentators label the word *arise* in this verse *"THE CALL"* and believe that this *call*, which was delivered through Moses to the children of Israel in Egypt, resounded again and again throughout Israel's history, and will be heard one final time as it precedes our final redemption. *Arise!* Messiah is here.

Until that day, His Spirit *calls* us to come higher, to come out of ourselves, to trust Him for more, to come out of complacency and lethargy, and to take a stand for Him.

The Hebrew word for *rise up* in this verse is frequently used in martial contexts referring to *preparation for, engagement in, and victory in war.* Sometimes *koom* connotes *anticipated or realized victory. "If God is for us, who can be against us?"* (Romans 8:31).

This is the hour for the Bride of Messiah to hear and obey Song of Solomon 2:10. Our Beloved is calling forth an army of "bridal-souls." We can no longer afford to leave our armor on the floor in our room. We must arise and put it on, prepared for battle. Dressed in her armor, Messiah's Bride is beautiful in His eyes. She has been given *the belt of truth, the breastplate of righteousness, the shield of faith, the shoes of peace, the helmet of salvation, and the sword of the Spirit.* This armor is part of our bridal adorning.

My love and *my fair one*, in verse 10, are terms of endearment for the Bride. *My love* in Hebrew is *rayati,* which literally means *my companion or close friend. My fair one* in Hebrew is *yaphah,* which we have seen before in The Song. It means *bright and beautiful. Come* in the phrase *come away* is *halach,* which is a primary root which can mean *to walk, get away, depart, flow, follow, or march.*

Whatever the nuance of the meaning, the centrality of the message is clear. *Yeshua* beckons us to come higher, perhaps to walk in the Spirit more consistently or to walk in love in a greater way. There is much room for a greater walk of faith in all our lives and a need to walk *worthy of our calling* in the Beloved. We must move out of our comfort zone.

One step at a time is all He expects. Our steps of faith are as beautiful to our Lord as a child's first steps are to his parents.

A new adventure in God awaits us as *Yeshua* holds out His arms to us, urging us to come away.

Try to give Him some extra time today so that He can reveal some of His plans for *your* life.

Day 64

For, lo, the winter is past, the rain is over and gone. Song of Songs 2:11

The land of the Bible, Israel, is a land primarily of two seasons, winter and summer. The winter (late September to March) is a time of rain. Summer is a hot, sunny time. Winter is a growing season, and summer is a time of resting of the land. Although rain provides plants with the moisture they need to bring forth fruit, when it ceases, there's a sense of relief and gladness. Most of us prefer bright, sunny days to dark, rainy days. The Shulamite rejoices to hear the Beloved announce that the rain has ceased.

The time when the rain stops and summer begins in Israel is a time of great beauty and fruitfulness. During the period between Passover and Pentecost (*Shavuot*), the wheat crop is ripening and the fruit of the rest of the seven species of Israel (especially the grape and olive) is beginning to develop.

The word for *winter* in this verse is *s'thav,* which comes from an unused root meaning *to hide.* The *winter* seasons in our lives tend to be those times when the Lord seems more distant. Some days are dark. Rain falls. We get wet and are chilled to the bone. Adversity is our portion. Perhaps we experience the death of a vision we feel the Lord has given to us. *Winter* can be a difficult season for lovers of God. And yet, the Bible tells us in Ecclesiastes 3:1: *"To everything there is a season, a time for every purpose under heaven."*

There are seasons in God. We experienced a difficult *winter* season during 1993 when my husband filled in as interim Messianic Rabbi for our spiritual leader who became ill and took a sabbatical rest. Our *winter* season included juggling two ministries at once and trying to keep a congregation afloat, while enduring criticism, insecurities, and even slander from within the ranks. What a challenge! *Winter* is a dark season as you pass through it, but there is new life being prepared beneath the surface at the same time. It is a time of being *rooted and grounded in love* (Ephesians 3:17). While we labored to help until our rabbi could resume his duties, God was preparing great blessings for us. A harvest was on its way. Summer was just around the corner.

It's such a comfort to hear the words *over and gone*. In Song of Songs 2:11, they literally mean that *the rain departed, walked, or marched away*. This phrase reminds me of our annual visits to the pediatrician with my two boys. How we all love to the hear the words "it's all over" as the nurse deftly removes the needles from our sight. We feel the same way when the dentist says those words. *The rains* come in the form of trials, chastisements, spiritual silence, and many attacks; but God is faithful and *the rain* passes. We thank Him for never giving us more than we can bear!

The traditional interpretation of *winter* among Jewish commentators is the four-hundred years of Egyptian bondage. As The Song of Songs is read each Passover in Jewish homes around the world, Jews are encouraged to see themselves as having personally come out of this bondage. As Messianic Jews, we always try to emphasize the glorious truth that *we really have* come out of bondage: the bondage to sin and spiritual Egypt. *The winter* of our separation from the God of Israel ended when we applied the blood of the Passover Lamb by faith to the doorpost and lintels of our heart. God is no longer hidden from us. We have met Him personally!

Winter is ending for Jewish people all over the world as *Yeshua* is revealing Himself to them. This is an exciting day in which to serve the Lord. We have a word of comfort for God's people Israel: "*Winter* is over. Spring has come!" The prophet Isaiah expressed this truth beautifully: "'*Comfort, yes, comfort My people!' says your God. 'Speak comfort to Jerusalem, and cry out to her, that her warfare is ended, that her iniquity is pardoned; for she has received from the Lord's hand double for all her sins'"* (Isaiah 40:1-2). *"'For a mere moment I have forsaken you, but with great mercies I will gather you. With a little wrath I hid My face from you for a moment; but with everlasting kindness I will have mercy on you,' says the Lord, your Redeemer"* (Isaiah 54:7-8).

The same God who comforts Israel desires to comfort *you*. He is kind. He is merciful. He uses *winter* for our good and our growth, but He makes sure that spring (or summer) follows.

Day 65

The flowers appear on the earth...
Song of Songs 2:12

Since I was a little girl, flowers have been closely associated with love. My mother and dad met while she was working in her aunt's florist shop in Valhalla, New York. Our home was constantly filled with flowers. By the time I was five-years-old, I knew most of the flowers in our gardens by name. I watched my parents lovingly care for huge beds of geraniums, petunias, zinnias, and marigolds. Our spacious yard was adorned with rose arbors, wisteria bushes, lilacs, violets, lilies of the valley, forsythia, peonies, hydrangea, and others, the names of which I've forgotten. My mother cut flowers on a regular basis and made arrangements of them for our home. Their beauty gave an unspoken message of a great love.

My father liked orchids—*big* ones—the cattleya variety. For as long as I can remember, he made sure I had a big orchid at Easter time. He never missed an Easter. Even during the years when alcoholism held him in cruel bondage and he deeply resented sharing me with my husband, he still managed to get an orchid for me. In his final years, he even arranged delivery of the orchid so that I could have it for Passover, since he knew that we attended a Messianic synagogue and celebrated the resurrection at Passover time. I still have the last two orchid corsages I received from Daddy hanging on the bulletin board in my office.

My dad went to be with the Lord on January 20, 1993. As Passover approached that year, I began to talk to the only father I now had—my Father in Heaven. I reminded him of the orchids and wondered if He was going to continue the tradition. The day of the Passover *seder,* the doorbell rang.

An orchid! The card said that the orchid was from my Heavenly Father, via Neil, my loving husband. I was thrilled.

Just as flowers fade, so do memories. A year passed, and spring arrived once more. It was Passover, and we were scheduled to fly to Chicago for a large public *seder*. I wondered about the orchid, but said nothing. As I looked outside my office window, I noticed that our gardenia bush was about to bloom. The next morning two beautiful white flowers appeared. I cut them and greatly enjoyed their fragrance and simple beauty. We left for Chicago, had a wonderful *Pesach*, and returned to Fort Lauderdale a few days later.

In my office again, I spoke with the Lord and said something to this effect: "I'm not upset, Lord, but I'm very surprised at You. You're so wonderful at details, and *never* miss an appointment, and I really thought you'd remember an orchid this year, too!" It was silent in my office for a moment, and then a still, small voice spoke directly to my spirit. "Which do you like better, orchids or gardenias?"

I answered "gardenias" because I adore the fragrance and, of course, most orchids don't have any fragrance. Gardenias were also the first flowers I ever received from a young man, and I usually requested gardenia corsages when I attended proms.

Then the Lord said, "So why do you think I made a mistake? Suppose I decided to send you gardenias instead of orchids? How long does an orchid last? How long do you suppose you'll have gardenias?"

I had them for *months*, well into the summer. My home was constantly filled with gardenias. I had put God in a box, and decided how He should bless me. He had a far better idea than I had!

The following year, 1995, promised to be an exciting sequel. The day before we left for our public *seder* in Saint Petersburg, Florida, the gardenia bush was loaded with green buds and looked about a week away from blooming. I mentioned this to Neil who just shook his head. The next morning, Neil came running into our bedroom saying: "He's *so* faithful. He's so *faithful*." Neil had gone outside and, sure enough, one gardenia had bloomed that morning. I thanked the Lord, danced around a bit, and carefully packed it in a cooler chest for the trip. The following night at the *seder*, I was seated at the piano playing some music as the guests were being seated, when Dennis, a thirteen-year-old boy who has watched us on television for many years, came up to me with a big plastic box. You guessed it! Inside was a big white orchid. I was speechless. Dennis said: "I hope you like it. God told me to buy it for you." (Isn't God romantic!)

There's *no way* to measure the deep, deep, never-ending love of God. At this moment, I have an orchid in the refrigerator, and at least 50 gardenias on a bush. Consider sending flowers to someone. They minister love, and the Lord causes them to *"appear on the earth"* to remind us of His love for us.

Day 66

*The flowers appear on the earth; the time of the
singing of birds is come...* Song of Songs 2:12

There's more that the Lord wants us to know about the
flowers mentioned in verse 12. They begin appearing in
Israel as early as January and continue into the month of
June. The word for *flowers* used in this verse, *nitsanim*, is
related to the word *nissan*, which is the first month of the
year on the biblical calendar and means *blossom*.

On our March 1995 trip to Israel, we arrived just as the
almond blossoms reached their peak. The almond is the
first tree to flower in Israel in the spring. It has beautiful
pink and white blossoms, and when the wind blows, petals,
like falling snow, float gently to the ground. It is a gorgeous
sight to behold!

In ancient times, almond blossoms had a special religious
significance for the Hebrews. The word for almond is
shaked, which means *to hasten or to watch for*. There is a play
on words in Jeremiah 1:11-12 that is only understood as
we translate into Hebrew: *"Moreover the word of the Lord
came unto me saying: 'Jeremiah, what seeth thou?' And I said:
'I see a rod of an almond-tree [shaked].' Then said the Lord unto
me: 'Thou hast well seen; for I watch [shoked] over My word to
perform it'"* (MASORETIC TEXT).

The God of Israel is ready to perform His word in each of
our lives! May the almond blossoms and all flowers remind
us of that truth. The Lord desires to send His word and heal
our loved ones. He longs to establish each of us in His Word
so that we can stand firm in the day of testing. He wants us
to claim the promises of His Word. They are God's "yes" to
us!

Messiah's Bride is ready for a new step in God. It is time for the Word to become flesh in her, to blossom forth in her daily life. What the Lord has worked *in* her must now be worked *out* in the presence of all people.

It is also time to *sing*. The Hebrew in this verse seems to indicate that *the singing* is not the *singing of birds* only. It is a time of *singing*, a time of praise. *Singing* praise to the Lord is always in order! I have especially enjoyed the last two years of praising the Lord in my living room with the company of a parakeet. The Bible says that everything that has breath should praise the Lord. We could take some lessons from the birds. *Singing* is a part of their being. It should be a part of ours, too.

Rashi, a famous Rabbinic commentator, says the phrase "the time of singing has come" could also be expressed "the time when you are destined to sing a song praising God for splitting the sea." We as believers in *Yeshua* have so much to sing about. We would have reason to *sing* if the Lord had only saved us from our sin. We have even more reason to *sing* since He saved us from our sin and put His Spirit within us. We have still more reason to *sing* since He saved us, sanctified us, and gave us His Word, the Holy Scriptures. And on top of all that, Messiah still intercedes for us daily and is preparing a place for us so that we can be with Him forever. *Dayenu!* This is more than enough reason to *sing* the praises of our God!

Passover, in traditional Judaism, is indeed a *time for singing*. Songs are sung throughout the *seder*, and in some homes, the *seder* concludes with many songs from the *Hallel* Psalms (Psalms 113-118).

Israel sang on the other side of the Red Sea. Can we do any less? Each year at Passover we sing a song of victory based on the Song of Moses from Exodus 15:1-2:

I will sing unto the Lord,
For He has triumphed gloriously
The horse and rider thrown into the sea.
The Lord, my God, my strength, my song
Has now become my victory.
The Lord is God and I will praise Him,
My Father's God and I will exalt Him!

Yeshua is our song. He is our strength. He is our victory. I WILL *sing*. It is an act of the will. We should *sing* to the Lord and praise Him at all times.

Our names are written in Heaven. That's reason to rejoice and to *sing*.

Our God loves us. That's another reason.

It's springtime for the soul. *SING.*

Day 67

...and the voice of the turtle[dove] is heard in our land.　　　Song of Songs 2:12

The Hebrew word *tor* is the word used here. It means *turtledove*. It is also a term of endearment. *Turtledoves* were part of the Old Covenant sacrificial system. They were often brought to the Jewish priest in pairs and became an offering made by fire, a sweet aroma to the Lord. The poor who could not afford a lamb usually brought *turtledoves* both as sin offerings and as burnt offerings. The Lord was pleased with this sacrifice. When the infant Jesus was presented to the Lord at the Temple in Jerusalem, Mary and Joseph brought a pair of *turtledoves* to offer according to the law of the Lord.

Today in Israel, there is talk about the reestablishment of the sacrificial system. There is an institute in Jerusalem which is actively preparing for the rebuilding of the Third Temple and the reinstatement of the sacrificial system. Someone in Israel is probably raising millions of *turtledoves* at this very moment. We have personally seen one of the silver vessels which have been created to catch the blood of the sacrifices. Will sacrifices begin again? If they do, God will not accept them. *The* sacrifice has already been made, for all men, for all time.

Yeshua, Jesus, like a *turtledove*, offered Himself to God as the final sacrifice for sin. The voice of His Spirit can be heard in Israel as never before. This voice is heralding the soon coming (the return) of the Messiah. Even Hasidic Jews with a Messianic fervor have hung up yellow signs all over Israel which say: **"Prepare for the coming of the Messiah."** Jewish believers in *Yeshua* are going out into the streets of Tel Aviv, Haifa, Jerusalem, and other cities, proclaiming the

Good News of *Yeshua*'s sacrifice for sin. They are modern-day *turtledoves* who have made great personal sacrifices to be the Lord's end-time messengers in His Land. Satan, and the ultra Orthodox community, would like to silence these voices, but they won't be able to. The voice of these *turtledoves* is part of a great divine plan.

The voice of the Spirit of God speaks to the hearts of men, women, and children all over the world, but there's something special about hearing this voice in God's favorite city, Jerusalem. On our first trip to Israel, Neil and I looked forward with great anticipation to going to the *Kotel* (Western Wall). We were surprised at how huge it is. Neil went to pray on the men's side, and I found a place on the women's side of the Wall. I sensed the presence of the Lord in a beautiful way and was moved to tears. Neil actually heard God's voice speak a powerful message to him as he watched the doves that make their home in the crevices of the wall. The Lord said, "My Spirit can go anywhere in the world He wants to but one place: the human heart. There, He must be invited in."

How God respects our free will! He won't force us to love Him or obey Him or seek His face. God is only glorified when we choose to make Him a priority in our lives and respond to His voice.

We can be *turtledoves* for our God. Let us offer Him *the sacrifice of praise* today, and present our bodies *as living sacrifices, acceptable to the Lord, which is our reasonable service.*

$\mathcal{D}ay$ 68

The fig tree putteth forth her green figs...
Song of Songs 2:13

The fig tree, t'aynah in Hebrew, has a prominent place in both the Old and New Covenant Scriptures. There were *fig trees* in the Garden of Eden. Adam and Eve sewed *fig* leaves together to cover themselves. The land that God promised His people in Deuteronomy 8:8 was *"a land of wheat and barley, of vines and FIG TREES and pomegranates, a land of olive oil and honey."*

The fig tree is seen as a prophetic timepiece in Scripture: *"Now learn this parable from the fig tree: When its branch has already become tender and puts forth leaves, you know that summer is near"* (Matthew 24:32). The *fig tree*, in this verse, is a symbol for Israel. This nation is God's timepiece. Bible prophecies are being fulfilled daily in the Land of Israel, as Jews are regathered to this land from the four corners of the earth. A close watch on Israel lets us know where we stand in God's prophetic plan.

In Song of Songs 2:13, *the fig tree* has green figs. These are figs which are not ripe. The tree is just beginning to bear fruit. Green figs are the promise of good things to come. *Figs* have an unusual habit of producing fruit before the leaves have emerged from the dormant period. When new leaves are fully out, the *fig* fruit is usually ripe. In this respect, *figs* produce their fruit in reverse of the pattern of most fruit trees. Israel will do something similar. Salvation came to her first, but she will bear fruit last. Fruit has come forth from the gentile church for almost two thousand years. Now Israel is beginning to bear fruit as *the fig tree* is firmly planted in her own land.

Israel is blossoming both physically and spiritually.

151

Fruits of all types are being grown very successfully in Israel and then shipped around the world in fulfillment of Isaiah 27:6: *"... Israel shall blossom and bud, and fill the face of the world with fruit."* Israel is bearing spiritual fruit as well. Wise soul-winners are producing what Proverbs 11:30 calls *"the fruit of the righteous,"* a *"tree of life"* — Jewish people who are receiving Jesus as their Messiah.

What should the church's relationship be to this budding *Fig Tree*? One of my favorite verses relevant to this question is found in Proverbs 27:18: *"Whoever keeps the fig tree will eat its fruit..."* This is a promise to those who bless Israel and the Jewish people. I often say that each time I am a blessing to my Jewish husband, there is the promise of fruit! Since being called into Messianic Ministry (beginning in 1976), I have been privileged to be a part of God's special plan to love, nourish, educate, encourage, exhort, and bless Israel. Oh, what blessings this has brought into my life! I'm sure that "keeping *the fig tree*" brings the same spiritual rewards as Genesis 12:3 and Psalm 122:6: *"I will bless those who bless you [Israel], and I will curse him who curses you..."* *"Pray for the peace of Jerusalem: May they prosper who love you."*

Remember in Song of Songs 2:10 when the Bridegroom calls to the Bride: *"Rise up, or Arise, my love"*? Part of this call concerns the Bride's relationship to the Bridegroom. Another part concerns the Bride's relationship to Israel. Consider the following verse from Psalm 102:13: *"You will arise and have mercy on Zion; for the time to favor her, yes, the set time, has come."*

Pray for Israel and her people today. This tiny nation is surrounded by enemies whose goal is her destruction. But God has another plan. Israel shall live and be made ready to welcome the King of kings and Lord of lords. It is God who has planted *The Fig Tree,* and what He does is forever.

Day 69

*...the vines with the tender grape give a good
smell...*   Song of Songs 2:13

If *the fig tree* represents Israel, *the vines* represent believers
in Messiah (the Church, the Bride, the Body). There's not
only fruit on *the fig tree*. There's also fruit on *the vine*.

There are many verses in the Bible that juxtapose *the
vine* and *the fig tree*. Together they symbolize peace, plenty,
prosperity, and security. Let's look at a few of these verses:

> *And Judah and Israel dwelt safely, each man under his
> vine and his fig tree, from Dan as far as Beersheba, all
> the days of Solomon.*   (1 Kings 4:25)

> *'In that day,' says the Lord of hosts, 'Everyone will
> invite his neighbor under his vine and under his fig
> tree.'*   (Zechariah 3:10)

> *But everyone shall sit under his vine and under his fig
> tree, and no one shall make them afraid; for the mouth
> of the Lord of hosts has spoken.*   (Micah 4:4)

One day, God's covenant people, both Israel and the
Church, will experience what is spoken of in these verses.
The vine and *the fig tree* will come together in oneness in the
Spirit of God. We have the same love. There is only one God.
There is only one Messiah. He called Himself *The Vine*.

In the *Tanach*, Israel is also referred to as *a vine*, but a
greater vine is found in the New Covenant in the person of
Yeshua of Nazareth who calls Himself *The True Vine*:

I am the true vine, and My Father is the vine-dresser. Every branch in Me that does not bear fruit He takes away; and every branch that bears fruit He prunes, that it may bear more fruit.

Abide in Me, and I in you. As the branch cannot bear fruit of itself, unless it abides in the vine, neither can you, unless you abide in Me. I am the vine, you are the branches. He who abides in Me, and I in him, bears much fruit; for without Me you can do nothing (John 15:1-2, 4-5).

John 15 is one of the most beautiful chapters in all of Scripture. The desire of the heart of God for UNION with us is overwhelming. So is our high calling to *BEAR FRUIT*.

If *Yeshua* is *the vine* and we are *the branches*, then *the fruit* on *the branches* is part of *the vine*. I think of John chapter 15 each time I hear someone chant the traditional blessing over the wine at *Shabbat* services, Passover *seders,* weddings, etc.: *"Baruch Atah Adonai Eloheinu Melech HaOlam, Boray Pre' Hagafen (Blessed Art Thou O Lord our God, King of the Universe who creates the fruit of the vine)."*

What is *the fruit of the vine*? Not just grapes. It is *US* — our lives in *Yeshua* as we abide in the Vine. It is the fruit of God's Spirit in us, His love, joy, peace, and more. *He* creates the fruit. We don't. We can't do anything without Him.

Messiah's Body has tender grapes today. Fruit is bursting forth. Believers are beginning to seek the Lord for a holier walk. Love for the Lord is being rekindled. Passion for souls is beginning to stir. And God is pruning us. Let us not recoil from this necessary part of the fruit-bearing process! Love prunes.

The fragrance of *the vine* is a delight to the senses. I remember playing near the huge grapevine that grew at the border of our property behind the garage. Especially when the grapes were ripe, the fragrance was so strong and sweet that I can remember it to this day.

We, Messiah's Bride, *"...are to God the fragrance of Messiah among those who are being saved and among those who are perishing"* (2 Corinthians 2:15).

The Lord even loves how we smell, because the fragrance of His Son's sacrifice clings to us as we cling to *Yeshua*. Hallelujah! Walk in that knowledge today.

Day 70

...Arise, my love, my fair one, and come away.
Song of Songs 2:13

The Bridegroom here repeats His call of Song of Songs 2:10 where He called to His Bride and told her that winter was over and spring had come. It was time to sing love songs and hear them from the lips of the Beloved. A time of fruitfulness had arrived, as well as a time in which God's Spirit was moving and Messiah's voice was heard in the land.

This was not the time to sit back and be satisfied with the status quo. God was on the move! She must arise and follow!

Have you ever prayed for the strength to endure your blessings? We have many times. We have found that with privilege comes responsibility. With promotions come additional yokes. With parenting comes pain. With prosperity comes additional pressure. With election comes persecution. Many of us can relate to Tevye in *Fiddler on the Roof* who said to God, "Couldn't you choose someone else for a change?"

Change is not popular with people. It is always unnerving, and we generally resist it, especially change in ourselves. But change is a fact of life in the Kingdom of God. In order for a Bride to be prepared for *Yeshua*, there must be change. When our Lord desires to see change in our lives, He calls us to *arise*.

We have often experienced the ambivalence of rejoicing in His call yet being somewhat reluctant to make a move. That's where *faith* enters. I'm sure it wasn't easy for Abraham to leave his family and the only home he knew to venture out into the unknown. He arose by faith. We have personally experienced this kind of change and step of faith many times since responding to the initial call of the Messiah in 1973.

Yeshua said, *Arise,* and we left home and family in New York and moved to Florida. He said, *Arise,* again, and we left teaching to enter the ministry full-time. Another *Arise* found us leaving our little townhouse in Davie, Florida, and moving into a huge house on Fort Lauderdale Beach — perhaps our biggest step of faith ever. This particular call, although glorious, included losing our privacy and welcoming over sixty-five people into our house to live with us over a period of eleven years.

In those eleven years, we heard *Arise* more than we ever wanted to hear it, as the Lord used Holy Spirit sandpaper on us to rub off our many rough edges (a practice He still continues).

We didn't hear the Lord say *Arise* at the *biggest change* in our lives — when I became pregnant for the first time at age 38 — but this too was part of God's special plan for our lives. There was yet another *Arise* when I became pregnant with my second child at age 41, and the Lord called us out of the beach house and into a family neighborhood in Plantation, Florida.

Sometimes the *Arise* has been heart-wrenching as we've heard the call to travel to minister somewhere as a couple, leaving the children behind as very little ones. They never seem to have suffered, but we have! "More faith, Lord! You say that *the just shall live by faith.*"

Our entire ministry stepped out by faith as *Yeshua* said *Arise* in December 1994 as we moved from our tiny space in the Temple Aron HaKodesh building to our own office on Oakland Park Boulevard in Fort Lauderdale.

We had needed to make the move for months since there wasn't enough space to even move in the old office. But Neil waited until he heard the Lord say, *"Arise, and come away."* At His Word, we stepped out. In our new facility, we saw the fruit of obedience and faith. A glorious coming-together happened before our eyes. *The vine* and *the fig tree* were both blossoming. A vision of what it means to be "One in the Messiah" became more and more real. Glory to God!

Perhaps God is calling you to *Arise*. Change is on the horizon. Don't be afraid. Trust His leading. Have faith in the One who is wonderfully faithful. Pray. Wait on Him. As you feel His leading, take a step of faith. Arise!

God will be pleased!

Day 71

O my dove, that art in the clefts of the rock, in the secret places of the stairs...

Song of Songs 2:14

Our Lord affirms us and praises us as we hearken to His call to arise. The term of endearment which He uses here for His beloved is *My dove, yonati* in Hebrew. The Shulamite is called Solomon's *dove before* she is called his *bride.* He is pleased that He detects the presence of His Spirit in her. Her position in Him also delights His heart. Where is she? Hidden *in the clefts of the rock.* This is where she should be! This is where doves nest.

We were made to hide ourselves in God. This is our position of security, rest, and intimacy. It is from this position that we arise to do exploits in *Yeshua.* I've always loved Colossians 3:3, as it so succinctly explains our position in Messiah: *"For you died, and your life is hidden with Messiah in God."* I never noticed until today, however, that this verse in Colossians follows two verses which deal with "arising." Here they are: *"If then you were RAISED with Messiah, seek those things which are above, where Messiah is, sitting at the right hand of God. Set your mind on things above, not on things on the earth."* We are able to hide our life in God because our real life is our *new* life in *Yeshua.* We are risen with Him. We dwell in *"...the secret place of the Most High"* (Psalm 91:1).

We are a Bride who was taken from the side of *the cleft Rock* (our crucified Messiah) just as Eve was taken from Adam's side. How is *Yeshua* a "cleft rock"? First of all, He is our Rock, the same Rock that followed the children of Israel in the wilderness, identified as Messiah in 1 Corinthians 10:4. When was the Rock split? When *Yeshua* died; a Roman soldier pierced His side with a spear and blood and water came out. From the wounded side of *Yeshua*, God the Father brought forth a Bride. That Bride is each of us when we are restored to God through faith in Messiah's atoning sacrifice. Then we are brought back under the arm of our Lord, close to His heart, sheltered, and protected.

God as *the Rock* has inspired songs throughout the centuries. *Maoz Tzur* (Rock of Ages) is a famous Jewish song usually sung at *Hanukkah* which extols God and His saving power. *Rock of Ages* is a famous Christian hymn which very possibly drew inspiration from The Song of Songs. It begins:

> *Rock of Ages, cleft for me,*
> *Let me hide myself in Thee.*

Those are powerful words, a cry from the heart of one who belongs to the King and longs to abide in Him.

What are *the secret places of the stairs*? Stairs go up. We ascend on stairs. Stairs speak of access, of approaching. The steps in *the Rock,* spoken of in this verse, are high above the ground, where eagles fly, where doves nest, like the *heavenly places* spoken of in Ephesians 2:6. We *are seated in heavenly places in the Messiah* and yet there's a progression of growth and maturity in *Yeshua* that leads us up a staircase.

There's an excellent commentary on The Song of Songs by Wade E. Taylor called *The Secret of the Stairs.* In his book, Dr. Taylor points out that there are two parts to stairs: a vertical part (riser) and then a platform. In the spiritual realm, the vertical part represents revelation. God through His Spirit speaks to our hearts, kisses us, and shows us a new truth about Himself, about His Word, or about His Kingdom. The platform is when we embrace what God has shown us and allow the Word to become flesh in our lives. This is how we grow in the Lord and ascend to the highest and best that He has for us, one step at a time.

When God gives you revelation, it is wise to ponder it in your heart until it becomes part of your experience, until you have walked in it. Then, and only then, will it minister life to others.

God has so much for each of us! We are His *dove*. He is our hiding place. The cleft Rock is our place of refuge and revelation where we can have peace in the midst of the storm, freedom from fear, and confidence in the day of trouble.

The hidden life is a position of power from which we can boldly proclaim: *"He is my defense; I shall not be greatly moved..."* (Psalm 62:2).

Day 72

...let me see thy countenance, let me hear thy voice; for sweet is thy voice, and thy countenance is comely.   Song of Songs 2:14

The Bridegroom now expresses His desire to see the face of His beloved dove and hear her voice. He tells her that her face is *beautiful* (comely) and her voice is *sweet*. He seeks a face-to-face relationship with her. This is a direct answer to her cry of Song of Songs 1:2. He desires to kiss her as much (or more) than she desires to be kissed.

The order in this verse is meaningful to me. Our Heavenly Bridegroom wants to see us, and *then* hear from us. This speaks about waiting on the Lord in prayer and communing with Him by spending time in His presence. If you were granted the privilege of an audience with an earthly king, you wouldn't enter his chambers and begin chattering away. You would wait until the time was right to speak. There would be a sense of awe and respect at just being in the king's presence. This is how it should be in our relationship with the King of kings. Our time with Him should include a lot of listening and silence. This is how I learned to distinguish the voice of the Lord from all the other voices around me.

There was a time in my early walk with the Lord that I began my private time with Him by listening to praise and worship tapes. I would meditate on the lyrics and think about the character of the Lord. Then I would read the Bible, a little at a time, and ponder the words carefully, slowly, in bite-size pieces. In this way I gave the *Ruach HaKodesh* time and opportunity to reveal truth to me. Sometimes I would cry. Sometimes I would laugh for joy. Many times I would lift my face to the Lord and just worship Him for who He is.

All this was done without using many words. My heart and my spirit were communing with the Holy One.

Our countenance is *comely* (lovely) to the Lord, no matter how it may seem to anyone else, including ourselves. Psalm 34:5 says that when we look to the Lord, we are radiant! Another verse from the Psalms has meant a lot to me over the years because it speaks about God being the health or help of our countenance. In both Psalm 42 and 43 we read the following: *"Why are you cast down, O my soul? And why are you disquieted within me? Hope in God; for I shall yet praise Him, the help of my countenance, and my God."* It is interesting to note that *health* or *help*, in these two Psalms, is actually *yeshua* in the Hebrew. Literally, God is the salvation or deliverance of our countenance.

When Neil was attacked with a terrible, deep fungus infection on his face in 1995, I reminded the Lord of this verse and claimed deliverance for my husband. Our faithful intercessors (Prayer Roses) also prayed for him, and the Lord healed his condition. Truly the Lord is our salvation — even the salvation of our face!

As we lift our countenance to Him, He lifts up His countenance upon us and grants us His peace (Numbers 6:26).

Once we have gazed upon the beauty of our Lord, basked in His presence, and just waited on Him, it is time to speak. What do you say to a King? You say whatever is on your heart. I've found that at this point, *Yeshua* is just delighted that you're with Him. He already knows your thoughts, your needs, your desires. Don't forget repentance and confession of sin. This assures an open channel of communication with the Lord. You can tell Him everything and He sees beyond it all. He is so wonderful.

The sweetness of our voice to the ears of our Lord can be compared to the delight of a parent at the sound of his or her child's "baby voice." Neil and I even put Jonathan's and Jesse's voices on tape because we knew the sweet baby quality would be short-lived. Expressions such as "tank you," "pease," "youtside," "happy to you," and "play toy" were precious to us. Our hearts melted when our children said: "I wuv you, Dada," or "I want Mama" (Jesse's first sentence). It didn't take much to please us. And it doesn't take much to please the Lord.

He just loves to see your countenance and hear your voice as you care enough to spend time with Him.

Day 73

Take us the foxes, the little foxes, that spoil the vines...   Song of Songs 2:15

The closer we draw to our Messiah, the more obvious and glaring our sins become. It is in the presence of God's dove-like Spirit that we perceive *little foxes*. The juxtaposition here of *doves* (verse 14) and *foxes* (verse 15) is interesting. I can't think of a better pair of opposites. We know that the *dove* is both symbolic of the *Ruach HaKodesh* and the Bride of Messiah who has that Spirit dwelling inside of her. What does she have to do with *foxes*? She has to war with them!

Foxes do not go away when we receive *Yeshua* as our Messiah, in much the same way that the Amorites, Canaanites, etc., did not go away when God brought the children of Israel into the Promised Land.

"But if you do not drive out the inhabitants of the land from before you, then it shall be that those whom you let remain shall be irritants in your eyes and thorns in your sides, and they shall harass you in the land where you dwell" (Numbers 33:55). These were the words of the Lord to Moses, but they could just as easily be the words of the Lord to us concerning *the little foxes*. God gives us the power to defeat them and is glorified when we do.

The Bridegroom is encouraging His Bride to join Him in the war against *the little foxes*. He's saying, in essence, "Let's take care of these little problems that are potentially very dangerous." Before we consider what these little problems might be, let's look at the *fox* for a moment.

The *fox* is a sly, quick, and destructive animal. *Foxes* were very common in the land of Israel at the time of *Yeshua*. They were particularly fond of grapes and would sneak into vineyards and destroy the entire crop. In Luke 13:32, the

Messiah calls Herod a *fox. Foxes* are symbolically enemies of God and His people.

In The Song, *little foxes* represent little sins in our lives. They are vestiges of the old self-life. They are hindrances to our spiritual growth, and we must do something about them. *Yeshua's "Take us the foxes"* or "Let's take the foxes" is similar to the Lord's plea in Isaiah 1:18: *"... let us reason together..."* Both refer to sin. Sin must be dealt with if we are to go on with the Lord.

There are three categories of *little foxes*:

(1) The wrong we think (heart sins). These are secret sins for the most part. Included in this group are attitudes such as pride, bitterness, unforgiveness, jealousy, anger, compromising, lust, defensiveness, and worry.

(2) The wrong we say (lip sins). An unruly tongue is the problem here—lying, criticism, gossip, slander, belittling, and complaining.

(3) The wrong we do (behavioral sins). Unloving actions are manifest in our lives. We are unkind, selfish, lazy, self-indulgent, unfaithful, rebellious, manipulating, and controlling.

Little foxes don't stay little for long. If you feed them, they grow. If you pet them, they stick around. If you stroke the *little fox* of feeling sorry for yourself, it can grow into an ugly spirit of self-pity. A little exaggeration here and there can evolve into a full-blown lying spirit. *Little foxes* are serious business!

In the 1980s, on the way to a seminar about deliverance, the Lord gave me a "kiss" from Psalm 97:10: *"You who love the Lord, hate evil!"* I knew the Lord was speaking to me about my attitude toward sin and unrighteousness. He was telling me that I was too tolerant, too laid back, too accepting of sin. This included the sin in me as well as the sin around me. He showed me that until I came to *hate* sin, I wouldn't be delivered of it. So we must ask ourselves: "Do I hate my self-sufficiency, my anger, my pride, my critical spirit, my carelessness, my unruly tongue, enough to be delivered from it?" We must be militant, violent, and determined when it comes to *little foxes*.

First of all, they must be recognized for what they are. Ask the Holy Spirit to reveal any *little foxes* in your life. Or, if you're very brave, ask your husband, wife, children, parents, or others close to you. Determine to deal with the *little foxes* with the Lord's help. Declare war on them. Don't feed or pet them! Hate them! Starve them to death! Fasting is a good weapon to use in the war against *little foxes*. Feed the spirit, deny the flesh, confess your sin, and use *the sword* (the Word of God) to slay *the little foxes*. Remember 1 John 1:9 as you make spiritual housecleaning a priority: *"If we confess our sins, He is faithful and just to forgive us our sins and to cleanse us from all unrighteousness."* Messiah will give you the victory over the little foxes!

$\mathscr{D}ay$ 74

...our vines have tender grapes.
Song of Songs 2:15

The promise of fruit is held forth in verse 15. The Bride of *Yeshua* was chosen to bear fruit: sweet, luscious, lasting fruit. *Little foxes* steal fruit. Just as a little bit of leaven can leaven a whole lump, a *little fox* can spoil an entire vine. *Little foxes* creep in unnoticed and destroy vines in blossom. The fruit is "nipped in the bud" before it can even burst forth in all its ripeness and beauty as God intended.

Our enemy, Satan, is interested in stopping us in the springtime of our love and resolve to follow after Messiah. His goal is *to steal and destroy*. He often does this by deceiving. He helps us to rationalize our sin ("I'm just made that way as a person"), to mislabel our sin ("I have a problem with people like that"), to make light of our sin ("The Lord understands my weakness in that area"), and to be unaware of it altogether ("Who me, a gossip?"). We need to ask the Lord for wisdom and discernment. We need to always know the truth. *Yeshua* is the Truth. He will show us the way.

"Vines with tender grapes" brings to my mind two groups of people in the Kingdom: new believers and children. Both of these groups are particularly targeted by Satan. If he can stop them at the beginning of their lives in the Lord, he has won a major victory. I am reminded of the time the enemy came against Jewish infants in an attempt to nip the Jewish nation in the bud (before the fruit, *Yeshua*, came forth). This occurred at the time of the Egyptian Pharaoh who was concerned with the blossoming of the Hebrew *vine* in his land. He ordered that all the Jewish male babies be cast into the river. As you recall, one of the Hebrew babies, Moses, was saved by Pharaoh's daughter and raised in the king's palace.

There is a story in the *Midrash* (rabbinic writings concerning the interpretation of biblical texts) about many of the other babies who were not saved. According to this tale, the Jewish women, in order to avoid Pharaoh's harsh decree, would hide their infant sons in basements. The wicked Egyptians would take their own young children into the Jewish houses and pinch them to make them cry. In response to these cries, the Jewish babies would start to cry, and their hiding places would be discovered, resulting in their being cast into the river. In this case, the *little* Egyptian *foxes* were used to help *spoil* the tender blossoms of the Jews.

Children continue to be the target of the enemy today. While young, tender, and impressionable, the evil one seeks to poison their little minds, especially via television and the media: "It's just a cartoon, Mama;" "It's not real;" "It's not that violent;" and "We're not going to do that to anybody" are some of the pro-television statements our boys have made to us. While their television viewing is very limited, we are still concerned with their exposure to values which are drastically different from ours. We are constantly asking the Lord for help in being watchmen and caretakers of *His vines*. We ask for wisdom and discernment in feeding, cultivating, and pruning so that fruit will be born in their lives.

In much the same way, new believers, as little children, need watchful care. It has been said that the first forty-eight hours are the most crucial. The enemy will attempt to come in and tell a new believer in Yeshua: "Nothing really happened when you prayed that prayer," or "It's all a fake," or "God will never accept you. You're not good enough." Follow-up is so important in these cases. So is discipleship. Little ones need to be nurtured. Fruit must be guarded.

At the time of *Yeshua*, a watchtower was built in a high, conspicuous spot in a vineyard. The tower's height enabled the watchman to oversee the entire vineyard to prevent theft from enemies, especially *foxes*. Those of us who are "higher up" (older) in the Kingdom have the responsibility of watching over the little ones.

Lord, please give us the grace, the strength, the wisdom, the ability, and the anointing to care for the tender little ones you send us.

Day 75

My beloved is mine, and I am his...
Song of Songs 2:16

The Shulamite responds to her Beloved with the first of three confessions about their relationship that occur in The Song. She says in Hebrew: *Dodi li va'ani lo* (*"My beloved is mine, and I am his."*). This is the exuberant confession of one who has found what he or she has been looking for their entire life. They've finally found it and are intent on keeping it. *It* (He) is their possession. There is also a sense, here, of the two-year-old who comes home from the toy store holding a bag with a new toy in it. His excitement vibrates from his entire body. If you ask him for the bag, he'll usually be quick to say: *"It's mine!"*

In this way, *Yeshua* belongs to young believers or old believers who are just entering a real "first love" experience with Him. We call this stage "*Me* first love." The Bride will eventually arrive at "*Him* first love" and finally progress to "*We* first love." But for now, what *He* is to her is foremost on the Shulamite's mind.

He is her atonement for sin.

He is her new life.

He is her forgiveness.

He is her total acceptance, her belonging.

He is her fulfillment as a person.

He is her love, joy, and peace.

He is hers.

Although somewhat immature and focused on self, this confession makes our Heavenly Father smile. He just loves the exuberance of the one who claims Him as his/her own. We often feel like locking away believers who can't stop talking about *Yeshua* until the honeymoon stage is over and

171

they calm down a bit. How wrong that would be! We need their fervor and their excitement about the Lord. It is a fresh wind blowing through the Body of Messiah. First love is very special.

I remember my days of teaching preschool right after accepting *Yeshua*. It was a wonder the other teachers and staff tolerated me. I was in a very secular environment and filled with the joy of the Lord. I gave God the glory for everything—the art projects I developed, the science experiments and cooking activities, a flourishing vegetable garden on the school grounds, whatever. I wasn't allowed to "preach," but I did lay hands on selected children and pray that they would grow up to be servants of the Lord. I made sure that all my students and parents knew who my Beloved was.

At one school, I was called to the office and told that I must be very careful not to use the name of Jesus because many of my students were Jewish and it would cause problems. So I said *God* instead, or "You know who," and they always knew! I'll never forget the day I took my kindergarten class to the lunchroom, and, before leaving them to go to the teachers' lunchroom to eat, I turned to them and said: "Now, I expect good behavior from all of you. I won't be here with you, but Someone is *always* watching you." Immediately, one of my most precious little Jewish girls screamed out in a very loud voice so that everyone in the cafeteria heard: "I know who it is teacher! It's Jeee-sus!" I smiled, turned red, and quickly exited the lunchroom.

When *Yeshua* is *ours*, we generally want Him to be everyone else's, too. In our zeal to share Him, my husband and I led at least thirty people to the Lord in the first year after receiving Him ourselves. Most of those are not walking with Him today. We had passion but no patience and about the same amount of wisdom. I would do things such as promising *Yeshua* four souls for His birthday and then do whatever I could to keep my promise.

In my diaries from these early years, I have found a beginning understanding of the second part of verse 16,

"I am his." To belong to *Yeshua* means that we no longer belong to ourselves. This is a big transition for most of us to make. On December 11, 1974, I wrote: "Jesus deals with me on giving. Can't hold back some for ourselves. I manage to let go."

Thank God He loves us in spite of our foolish, childish, self-centered ways! What a miracle it is to be able to claim the King of Glory as our own. We love Him, and He loves us. We have the sweet assurance that we belong to Him. Allow this truth to bless and comfort your heart today.

Day 76

...He feedeth among the lilies.
Song of Songs 2:16

Chapter 2 ends with a picture of Messiah as a Shepherd in the company of his pure-in-heart, *lily*-like sheep. The Hebrew word for *feedeth,* in verse 16, is the primary root *ra'ah,* which means *to tend a flock or pasture it.* It also includes the idea of *friendship.* In chapter 1, the Shulamite had asked where the Beloved fed His flocks. We began chapter 2 with the Shulamite calling herself a *lily of the valley* and the Bridegroom calling her a *lily among thorns.* The picture comes into focus for us now. The Bridegroom can be found among His friends, the *"lily*-souls." The words of *Yeshua,* as found in John 15:15, apply here: *"No longer do I call you servants, for a servant does not know what his master is doing; but I have called you friends, for all things that I heard from My Father I have made known to you."* A degree of intimacy has been reached here, a reciprocal love, a mutual sharing that indicates a step upward on the staircase of the bridal relationship.

Some Orthodox Jewish commentators translate *lilies* (*shoshanim*) as *roses.* They say that God rested His *Shechinah* upon Moses, Aaron, and the seventy Elders, who in the fragrance of their actions are compared to *roses. Roses,* in a more global sense, represent all those who are "righteous." God does indeed rest His *Shechinah* glory on the righteous today. Who are the righteous? The *lilies* (or *roses*) are the righteous. The Beloved made us that way: *"For as by one man's disobedience many were made sinners, so also by one Man's obedience many will be made righteous"* (Romans 5:19).

The Lord brought to my attention the other day a beautiful example of *Yeshua* feeding among the lilies. It happened to be the National Day of Prayer. I had been meditating on *lilies* during the day, and at night, while listening to the radio in our car on the way to the grocery store, the Lord gave me a kiss from Song 2:16. I tuned in to a "Concert of Prayer" at Moody Bible Church in Chicago, Illinois. It was a three-hour service in which Christian leaders of many denominations and nationalities from all over the country joined together to pray for our country. The presence of the Lord among His people could be felt over the airwaves. The unity of the Spirit must have been a joy to the Father's heart. The believers gathered in Moody Church were *lilies*. The Good Shepherd, Yeshua, the Messiah, was in their midst tending His flock.

It "just so happened" that I began listening to the program right before Joni Erickson Tada was asked to pray. She prayed right out of The Song of Songs, quoting many of the verses I had been reading as she prayed. How does the Lord do this? Yesterday, after writing on *little foxes*, I ran to pick up Jesse at school to take him to piano lessons. We put his Yamaha music school cassette tape into the cassette recorder in the car and a song we had never heard before came on. It was called *Little Foxes*. It must be obvious by now that I see God in *everything!*

And I see Him in a beautiful way among His people. Over the years (since 1973), Neil and I have had the privilege of attending or ministering in churches of many different denominations. We have also shared in home groups and fellowships of many types. It has been our great joy to experience oneness in the Lord with believers who love the Lord with all their heart. The differences in our theology have not interfered in the least with our unity in Messiah. Love has been the bond. From the Assemblies of God Church of our beginnings, to our Messianic Synagogue, various groups in Ecuador and Israel, and then Baptists, Methodists, Lutherans, Episcopalians, Black Pentecostals, Presbyterians, Disciples of Christ, Mennonites, and many interdenominational fellowships in this country, we have been "at home" with the people of God.

"For where two or three are gathered together in My name, I am there in the midst of them" (Matthew 18:20). He *feeds among the lilies.* We have the promise of His presence. Let us gather together with others who have the same love and give our Shepherd a great big collective hug. We can delight His heart. We can satisfy Him.

$\mathcal{D}ay$ 77

Until the day break, and the shadows flee away,
turn, my beloved, and be thou like a roe or
a young hart upon the mountains of Bether.
Song of Songs 2:17

"Not yet, Lord!" Satisfied with the goodness of the Lord and enjoying the fact that her Beloved is hers, the Bride has missed the point. She is called to follow, not to lead. We can't tell the Lord what to do. *He* is Lord. He calls His Bride to *arise*. If we fail to obey, we miss His best for us. We also miss the awareness of His presence.

This is one of the verses in The Song that is open to much discussion. The only *clear* part of the verse is the idea of "separation" or division. (*Bether* in Hebrew means *separation* or *division*.) There appears to be a separation between the Bride and the Beloved. The Beloved may have hidden Himself. Does God do this? Yes, according to Holy Scripture. Zephaniah 3:17 tells us that He is *"silent in His love"* (Amplified). Isaiah 8:17 says: *"And I will wait on the Lord, who hides His face from the house of Jacob; and I will hope in Him."*

Separation is a part or our growth in the Beloved. While it is true that He never leaves us nor forsakes us (Hebrews 13:5), there are times when the Lord deliberately withdraws the sense of His presence from us. He wants to help us grow out of our self-life into His life. He's not angry with us, and He hasn't left us. In His love, He is teaching and correcting us.

Sometimes we cause separation between ourselves and the Beloved. Have you ever said, "Later, Lord"? I have. The Shulamite tells the Beloved to wait until morning. Then she will follow. But He is calling her *now*. The day has already begun according to *His* timing. (On the Hebrew calendar, the day begins in the evening.) How hard it is for us to learn that God's ways are not *our* ways. His ways are much higher and better!

I am particularly guilty of saying "not now" to the Lord, especially when it comes to the early morning hours. I greatly admire those of you who rise before dawn to meet the Beloved. How He must love and appreciate you! It amazes me that the Lord is so gracious to me and meets with me when the sun is up. Though we are faithless, He remains faithful.

There is another way to look at this final verse of chapter 2. We can get a glimpse of the Shulamite's heart, calling to the Beloved to leap over any separation in their union, and return to her speedily. Until that glorious, eternal day, when we no longer see through a glass darkly, but see our Beloved face to face, and know Him as He knows us (1 Corinthians 13:12), we need His light to lighten our way, as the Shulamite needed Shlomo.

Our Beloved is in covenant with us. He is ours forever. We can depend on Him. The Hebrew word *be-ter* in this verse is the same word used in Genesis 15:10 to refer to a sacred covenant. The Lord told Abram to cut animals in two and arrange the halves in a certain way in preparation for a covenant that God was about to make.

Our God is a covenant-keeping God. Our Bridegroom-King, *Yeshua the Messiah, made a New Covenant through His own blood. Everything He has is ours. Nothing in this world can ever separate us from His love. Receive this truth from Romans 8:38-39 as your kiss today, cherish it, and repeat it often to yourself until your Heavenly Bridegroom returns for you:*

"For I am persuaded that neither death nor life, nor angels nor principalities nor powers, nor things present nor things to come, nor height nor depth, nor any other created thing, shall be able to separate us from the love of God which is in Messiah Yeshua our Lord."

Bibliography

Bloch, Ariel & Chana. The Song of Songs. (New York, N.Y.: Random House, Inc., 1995).

Burrowes, George. The Song of Solomon. (Carlisle, Pennsylvania: The Banner of Truth Trust, 1977). [First published 1853].

Cohen, Rev. Dr. A., Editor. The Five Megilloth. [The Soncino Books of the Bible]. (London: The Soncino Press, 1977).

Fruchtenbaum, Arnold G. Biblical Lovemaking. (San Antonio, Texas: Ariel Press, 1983).

Gordis, Robert. The Song of Songs. (New York, N.Y.: The Jewish Theological Seminary of America, 1954)

Guyon, Madame. The Song of Songs. (Augusta, Maine: Christian Books Publishing House, 1984).

Heydt, Henry. The King of Kings in The Song of Songs. (Orangeburg, N.Y.: American Board of Missions to the Jews, 1979).

MacIlravy, Cora Harris. Christ and His Bride. (Ashville, N.C. : Elbethel, A Christian Fellowship, 1916).

Nee, Watchman. Song of Songs. (Fort Washington, Pennsylvania: Christian Literature Crusade, 1965).

Penn-Lewis, Jessie. Thy Hidden Ones. (Bournemouth, Hants, England: The Overcomer Book Room, 1951).

Scherman, Rabbi N., and Zlotowitz, Rabbi Meir, Editors. Shir ha Shirim. [The Art Scroll Tanach Series] (Brooklyn, N.Y: Mesorah Publications, Ltd. 1977).

Shaw, Gwen. Song of Love. (Jasper, Arkansas: End-time Handmaidens, 1974).

Schlink, Basilea. My All For Him. (Minneapolis, Minnesota: Bethany House Publishers, 1971).

Swenson, Allan A. Plants of the Bible and How to Grow Them. (New York, N.Y.: Carol Publishing Group, 1994).

Taylor, J. Hudson. Union and Communion. (Minneapolis, Minnesota: Bethany Fellowship, Inc.).

Taylor, Wade E. The Secret of the Stairs. (Salisbury Center, N.Y.: Pinecrest Bible Training Center Publications, 1976).

Varner, Rev. Kelley H. Principles of Present Truth from Ecclesiastes and Song of Solomon. (Richlands, North Carolina: Praise Tabernacle Ministries, 1992).

Weiner, Bob & Rose. Bible Studies for the Preparation of the Bride. (Gainesville, Fl.: Maranatha Publications, 1980).

Wittich, Philip. An Exposition of the Song of Solomon, Vol. I. (No specifics given in book.).

Wurmbrand, Richard. The Sweetest Song. (Basingtoke, Hants RG23, 7LP, UK: Mashall Morgan and Scott Publications Ltd., 1988).

Write for your free catalog!

For additional materials by Jamie Lash
and a catalog of Messianic Jewish resource
materials, including teaching and music CDs,
DVDs, Judaica gift items and more, call:
1-800 2YESHUA or write to:

Jewish Jewels
P.O. Box 450550
Ft. Lauderdale, FL 33345-0550

✡ ✡ ✡

Complimentary Teaching Newsletter
available upon request!